How We Got Our Bible

HOW WE GOT OUR BIBLE

by

Ralph Earle

BAKER BOOK HOUSE
Grand Rapids, Michigan

Published 1971
by Beacon Hill Press
Kansas City, Missouri

ISBN: 0-8010-3271-7

Reprinted by Baker Book House

First printing, April 1972
Second printing, May 1973
Third printing, February 1975
Fourth printing, August 1977

PHOTOLITHOPRINTED BY CUSHING - MALLOY, INC.
ANN ARBOR, MICHIGAN, UNITED STATES OF AMERICA
1 9 7 7

Contents

Preface

One of the most heartening trends of the last 20 years has been the greatly increased interest in the study of the Bible. As far as we can discover, in the first 50 years of this century (1900-1949) there appeared only about half a dozen significant new series of English commentaries on the Bible (or New Testament). But in the next 10 years (1950-59) no less than 10 were begun. Here is a partial list:

1. "Bible Commentary" (Lutheran)
2. "Cambridge Greek Testament Commentary"
3. "Daily Study Bible" (William Barclay)
4. "Epworth Preacher's Commentaries"
5. "Evangelical Commentary on the Bible"
6. "Harper's New Testament Commentaries"
7. *Laymen's Bible Commentary*
8. "New International Commentary"
9. *New Testament Commentary* (William Hendriksen)
10. "Tyndale New Testament Commentaries"

During the next decade (1960-69) several other new series were started. These include:

1. "Anchor Bible"
2. *Beacon Bible Commentary*
3. "Cambridge Bible Commentary"
4. "New Clarendon Bible"
5. *Wesleyan Bible Commentary*

Some of these series (quotation marks) or sets (italics) run into many volumes. For instance, "The Anchor Bible"— the first such joint project of Catholics, Protestants, and Jews—is scheduled for 50 volumes.

Besides this, there is a host of briefer books on Bible study, most of them written by evangelicals. When we add to this the large crop of new translations of the Bible in our generation, it is easy to see that the Book of Books is being read and studied by myriads of people. For this we devoutly give God thanks.

In such a day as this a very basic question for all of us is: How did we get our Bible? This book seeks to answer that query, in a brief survey of the subject.

—RALPH EARLE

Glossary

Apocrypha—books in the Catholic Old Testament that are not in most of our Bibles today.

Canon—list of books of the Bible officially accepted by the Church.

Codex—a bound book, in contrast to a roll or scroll.

Dead Sea Scrolls—manuscripts, mostly biblical, discovered in caves near the Dead Sea.

Diaspora—the dispersion or scattering of the Jews beginning about 300 B.C.

Inquisition—a Roman Cathloic tribunal that suppressed heresy.

Manuscript—a handwritten copy of a book.

Massoretic Text—Hebrew text of the Old Testament edited by Jewish scribes of the Middle Ages.

Minuscules—Greek manuscripts of the New Testament written in the ninth to fifteenth centuries.

Papyrus—ancient "paper" used as writing material at the time of Christ.

Pentateuch—first five books of the Bible.

Peshitta—Syriac translation of the Bible.

Proselyte—convert to Judaism (or any other religion).

Septuagint—Greek translation of the Old Testament made about 250-150 B.C.

Targums—Aramaic paraphrases of the Old Testament.

Version—a translation of the Old or New Testament.

Vulgate—Latin translation of the Bible made in the fourth century.

Uncials—Greek manuscripts of the New Testament written in the fourth to ninth centuries.

Prologue

A lonely shepherd sat on the back side of the desert. All was still. No blaring radio, glaring television, ringing doorbell or telephone. No rumble of distant traffic or roar of jet piercing the sky. Not a sound shattered the silence; not a sight of moving man or beast greeted his eye.

A later psalmist was to write: "Be still, and know that I am God" (Ps. 46:10). In the stillness of that distant day a grateful shepherd met the Great Shepherd. From leading a few sheep of his father-in-law he was called to lead the large flock of God's people.

The solitude lent wings to his thoughts. He remembered the stories his devout mother had told him—of Adam and Eve, of Cain and Abel, of Noah and the Flood, of Abraham, Isaac, Jacob, and Joseph. Little did he realize that under the inspiration of the divine Spirit he would one day be the human instrument for preserving these stories for countless generations to come.

His mind went back over his own lifetime. A cruel Pharaoh had given orders to kill all the male children of Israel. But as a baby, Moses had been miraculously preserved from death. Adopted by Pharaoh's daughter, he had been brought up at the royal palace. There he was carefully educated "in all the wisdom of the Egyptians, and was mighty in words and in deeds" (Acts 7:22). Egypt was the greatest empire of that day and the leading center of learning. God was preparing His servant for his twofold task. The training he received as heir to the throne of the Pharaohs stood him in good stead when he became the founder of the new nation of Israel, and the schooling he had received in the greatest literature of that day was priceless in his preparation for becoming the first scribe of divine Scripture.

When Moses was 40 years old, he made a momentous decision. He would forsake the court of Pharaoh and cast his lot with his own persecuted people. He would deliver them from oppression and slavery.

But he made the mistake of attempting this in his own strength and wisdom. Discovering a poor Hebrew slave being beaten, Moses killed the cruel Egyptian and buried him in the sand. But Pharaoh heard about it and Moses had to flee for his life.

Forty years had passed since then. Frustrating as the seemingly endless time had been, Moses had learned some invaluable lessons of patience. But something else had happened. Far removed from palace intrigues and the petty bickerings of court life, the lonely shepherd had found an awareness of God's presence. Meditation became his most important vocation. He was learning much that was not in the wisdom books of Egypt.

Then another hour struck on the clock of the holy history. As Moses sat one day, watching his flock and meditating on the past, he noticed a bush burning nearby. Had the blazing sun ignited it? But why was the bush not consumed in the flames?

Curious, Moses stepped nearer for a better look at this strange sight. Then, out of the burning bush came the voice of God. The great "I Am" revealed himself as the God of Abraham, Isaac, and Jacob, and also as the Redeemer of Israel. Moses was called to be the messenger of God, delivering the Israelites from Egyptian bondage and giving them the divine law of Sinai. More than that, he was to record the story of creation and God's dealings with mankind. He was to write the first chapters of salvation history, the beginnings of our Bible.

I

Its Origin

Its Inspiration

There are two definite passages in the New Testament on the subject of inspiration. One is II Tim. 3:16—"All scripture is given by inspiration of God, and is profitable for doctrine, for reproof, for correction, for instruction in righteousness." The phrase "given by inspiration of God" is all one word in Greek, *theopneustos*—literally, God-breathed. That is, sacred Scripture was breathed out by God and breathed into men's minds by the Holy Spirit. Clement of Alexandria (2nd cent.) and Origen (3rd cent.) use this term to describe the Scriptures.

The second passage is II Pet. 1:21—"For the prophecy came not in old time by the will of man: but holy men of God spake as they were moved by the Holy Ghost." Literally the second half of this verse reads: "But being borne along by the Holy Spirit, men spoke from God." That is, the human writers of the Bible were lifted by the Holy Spirit to a higher level of spiritual understanding, so that they could receive divine truth and communicate it to their fellowmen.

James Arminius was a Dutch theologian who was born in 1560 and died in 1609. With regard to the Bible he wrote: "We now have the infallible word of God in no other place than in the Scriptures."[1] He goes on to make this helpful statement:

> The primary cause of these books is God, in his Son, through the Holy Spirit. The instrumental causes are holy men of God, who, not at their own will and pleasure, but as they were actuated and inspired by the Holy Spirit wrote these books, whether the words were inspired into them, dictated to them, or administered by them under divine direction.[2]

This passage suggests three degrees of inspiration for different parts of the Bible. First there is eternal truth—that could not otherwise be known by the human intellect— "inspired into"; that is, breathed out of God and into the hearts and minds of the writers. In the second place, some parts of the Scripture seem actually to have been dictated, as in the case of the law given to Moses at Sinai. But other parts of the Bible were simply "administered to them under divine direction." These would include the genealogical tables, as in the first nine chapters of I Chronicles, and other historical documents which the authors were led by the Spirit to incorporate in their writings.

It was John Wesley in the eighteenth century who took the theology of James Arminius and made it the powerful force for precipitating the greatest spiritual revival England has ever seen. In the preface to his *Explanatory Notes upon the New Testament* he says of sacred Scripture: "Every part thereof is worthy of God; and all together are one entire body, wherein is no defect, no excess."[3]

In the same connection he writes: "The language of His messengers, also, is exact in the highest degree: for

---

[1]*Writings*, trans. James Nichols and W. R. Bagnall (Grand Rapids: Baker Book House, 1956), II, 15.

[2]*Ibid.*, p. 16.

[3]*Explanatory Notes upon the New Teatament* (London: Epworth Press, 1941), p. 9.

the words which were given them accurately answered to the impressions made upon their minds."[4]

Commenting on II Tim. 3:16, Wesley writes: "The Spirit of God not only once inspired those who wrote it [the Scriptures], but continually inspires, supernaturally assists, those who read it with earnest prayer."[5]

The greatest Wesleyan theologian of the past was W. B. Pope. In his three-volume *Compendium of Christian Theology* (first published in 1875-76) he devotes 37 pages to the subject of the inspiration of the Bible. He writes of the Bible:

> Its plenary inspiration makes Holy Scripture the absolute and final authority, all-sufficient as the Supreme Standard of Faith, Directory of Morals, and Charter of Privileges to the Church of God. Of course, the Book of Divine revelations cannot contain anything untrue; but its infallibility is by itself especially connected with religious truth . . . It is after all, a Divine-human collection of documents: the precise relation of the human to the Divine is a problem which has engaged much attention, and has not yet been, though it may yet be, adequately solved. But in the domain of religious truth, and the kingdom of God among men, its claim to authority and sufficiency is absolute.[6]

The outstanding Arminian theology of this century was written by the late H. Orton Wiley. His definition of inspiration is as follows: "By *Inspiration* we mean the actuating energy of the Holy Spirit by which holy men were qualified to receive religious truth and to communicate it to others without error."[7]

[4]*Ibid.*

[5]*Ibid.*, p. 794.

[6]*A Compendium of Christian Theology* (2nd ed., New York: Phillips and Hunt, 1881), pp. 174ff.

[7]*Christian Theology* (Kansas City: Nazarene Publishing House, 1940), I, 168.

Wiley holds that the Bible was fully inspired. He says that the Scriptures were "given by plenary inspiration, embracing throughout the elements of superintendence, elevation and suggestion, in that manner and to that degree that the Bible becomes the infallible word of God, the authoritative Rule of Faith and Practice in the Church."[8]

Similar is the statement made by Adam Clarke, the leading Bible commentator of the Wesleyan movement. He says: "I only contend for such an inspiration of the sacred writers of the *New Testament,* as will assure us of the truth of what they wrote, whether by inspiration of *suggestion,* or *direction* only; but not for such an inspiration as implies that even their words were dictated, or their phrases suggested to them by the Holy Ghost."[9] This is a good description of what we mean by plenary dynamic inspiration.

A Divine-human Book

The Bible is a divine-human Book, as Christ is the divine-human Person. This is the key that unlocks the door to an understanding of the true nature of the Scriptures.

God could have sent His Son in adult human form without a human birth. Jesus' body would then have been simply a shell in which was encased the divine nature.

But God in His wisdom did not choose to do it that way. Rather, He caused His Son to be born of a woman. Jesus thus partook of the personality characteristics of His mother —psychologically as well as physically. He not only bore resemblance to her in His facial features but He was influenced by the intellectual and social atmosphere of the home. He was the son of Mary as well as the Son of God.

---

[8] *Ibid.,* p. 170.

[9] *The New Testament of Our Lord and Saviour Jesus Christ* (New York: Abingdon-Cokesbury Press, n.d.), I, 10.

So it was with the Bible. God could have sent down the Book all inscribed with the complete revelation, bound in black leather, divinity circuit, gold-edged, silk-sewn, India paper—even dedicated to King James! But He did not choose to do so. Instead the light of divine revelation broke in on the soul of Moses, of David, of Paul, of John, and many others. The result is a divinely inspired, humanly written Revelation of God's truth for man.

They wrote on sheepskin and goatskin, on papyrus and parchment. They wrote the thoughts of God as best they could understand them by the help of the Holy Spirit.

Just as sunlight when conducted through a prism is broken down into its various rays, so the light of God's truth when filtered through the prisms of human personalities took on the varying slants and interests of those personalities. That is shown not only in the language used— both vocabulary and style—but also in actual thought-forms, in ways of approach, in diversity of emphasis. The Holy Spirit used the varying interests and emphases of the different writers to convey the total of divine revelation in the Bible.

It is unfortunate that too often we see only one side of truth, and so we actually have only a half-truth. Ask an evangelical, "Was Jesus divine or human?" and he will answer emphatically, "Divine!" Ask a humanist the same question and the reply will be, "Human." Both are right and both are wrong. The opposition between Jesus' deity and humanity exists only in false theological thinking. Jesus was, and is, both human *and* divine.

The same situation obtains in relation to the Scriptures. Evangelicals emphasize the *divine* source of the Bible until they sometimes neglect the *human* origin. Liberals stress the latter and forget the former. The Bible did have a human origin; it came from the hands of the men who wrote it, but its ultimate source was divine; the Holy Spirit inspired the writers. It is this which gives it its unique authority as the Word of God.

One man sees only the scribe sitting as a desk, pen in hand, writing the words of scripture, and he declares, "The Bible is a human book." Another sees only the inspiring Spirit hovering overhead; and he cries, "It is divine!" What we need is to see the whole picture, not just one part of it. The Bible is a divine-human Book.

In the Preface to his sermons, John Wesley wrote these beautiful words:

> I have thought, I am a creature of a day, passing through life as an arrow through the air. I am a spirit come from God, and returning to God: Just hovering over the great gulf; till a few moments hence, I am no more seen; I drop into an unchangeable eternity! I want to know one thing,—the way to heaven; how to land safe on that happy shore. God himself has condescended to teach the way: For this very end he came from heaven. He hath written it down in a book. O give me that book! At any price, give me the book of God! I have it: Here is knowledge enough for me. Let me be *homo unius libri* [a man of one Book]. [10]

The Pages Appear

Morning dawned over the camp of Israel. Suddenly the silence of the disappearing night was shattered. Rumbling thunder roared overhead.

Nervously the people pulled aside their tent flaps and looked out just in time to see another blinding light streak across the sky. Now the lightning was flashing, and the thunder crashing. Out of the thick cloud that covered the top of Mount Sinai a trumpet blast came, loud and long. All the people stood in their tent openings, trembling with fear.

[10]*Works* (Kansas City: Beacon Hill Press, n.d.), V, 3.

As they looked up at the sacred mountain, smoke billowed from its peak as if from a giant smokestack, "because the Lord descended upon it in fire" (Exod. 19:18). It seemed now that the hill was one big, smoldering furnace. To add to the people's terror, the whole mountain shook with a violent earthquake.

But one man was unafraid, because he had met God at the burning bush, right in this same place (Exod. 3:2). So he called out, and God answered him (Exod. 19:19). Moses was summoned to the top of Mount Sinai. That day the Ten Commandments were given (Exodus 20). Israel was to be the people of the covenant, the people of the Book. And Moses was God's scribe, to give them the Book of the Law.

Traditionally the first five books of our Bible are assigned to Moses. For the material recorded in *Genesis,* Moses would have had to depend on oral traditions, handed down from generation to generation, and on the direct inspiration of the Holy Spirit. As far as the Genesis record of the creation of the world and of human life is concerned, this would all have had to be given by divine revelation, for no man was present to see these events and tell about them.

When it came to the materials of *Exodus, Leviticus, Numbers,* and *Deuteronomy,* Moses was the man most involved. No one could have written this down better than he.

It should be noted, however, that the last chapter of Deuteronomy was obviously not written by him. Here we find an account of Moses' death and burial, with the added statement: "But no man knoweth of his sepulchre unto this day" (Deut. 34:6). A further observation is made: "And there arose not a prophet since in Israel like unto Moses, whom the Lord knew face to face" (v. 10). To say that Moses himself wrote these words beforehand by divine inspiration—as some have claimed—is unrealistic. The whole tenor of the terminology used here clearly points to a later generation, when the monumental work of Moses was edited in its final form.

The Books Multiply

Joshua was Moses' successor, and the sixth book of our Old Testament is named for him. It records his great achievements in leading the Israelites across the Jordan River, conquering the land of Canaan, and assigning each tribe its territory. The book divides itself very naturally at the middle into two parts. The first (cc. 1—12) tells of the conquest of Canaan, the second (cc. 13—24) records the partition of the land.

The fact that Joshua's name is attached to the book does not mean that he wrote it. For in the last chapter we find the record of the death and burial of God's great warrior (Josh. 24:29-30). Then comes the statement: "And Israel served the Lord all the days of Joshua, and all the days of the elders that overlived Joshua" (v. 31). It is clear that, at least in its finished form, the Book of Joshua was written in a later generation. We do not know who wrote it.

The same must be said of the book of *Judges*, which fills in the time from Joshua to Samuel. The keynote of this book is: "In those days there was no king in Israel: every man did that which was right in his own eyes" (17:6; 21:25). With no central government, the Israelites too often lived in chaotic confusion. The recurring sequence in Judges is disobedience, oppression, repentance, and deliverance. The so-called "judges" were for the most part sent by God to deliver the people from their oppressors.

The little love story called *Ruth* gives a brief picture of life in that period (Ruth 1:1). Its purpose may have been at least partly to fill in one point in the ancestry of King David (Ruth 4:17-22).

The two books of *Samuel* cover the period of that great prophet and also the reigns of Saul and David, the first two kings of Israel—both of whom were anointed by Samuel. The narrative begins with the birth of this man (c. 1) and his call to the prophetic ministry (c. 3). He devoted a long lifetime to ruling Israel as a judge. Unfortunately, he failed to train his own children to follow in his footsteps (I Sam. 8:1-5). And so the people asked for a king. In answer to their plea, God instructed Samuel to anoint Saul as the first king over Israel. But Saul became stubborn and disobedient, and his life ended in disaster. The importance of David's reign is shown by the fact that the entire Book of II Samuel is devoted to it.

The two books of *Kings* describe the reign of Solomon over the united Kingdom of Israel—which had been carved out by his father, David—and also the period of the divided monarchy. The northern Kingdom of Israel was ruled by several dynasties, beginning with Jeroboam. It came to an end in 722/21 B.C. with the capture of its capital city, Samaria, by the Assyrians, and the deportation of the people to Mesopotamia (II Kings 17:6). To fill the vacancy, the king of Assyria brought people from the East and settled them in the cities of Samaria (II Kings 17:24). The result was the half-breed race of Samaritans in Jesus' day.

An interesting feature of the history of north Israel is the appearance of two unique prophets, Elijah and Elisha. They sought to call the idolatrous Israelites back to the worship of the true God, but with limited results.

The southern Kingdom of Judah was ruled by a single dynasty, that of David. It came to an end in 586 B.C. with the fall of Jerusalem to the Babylonians. Except for the 80 years of Maccabean independence (142-63 B.C.), there was no independent nation of Israel from 586 B.C. to A.D. 1948, when the new state of Israel was set up.

The observant reader may have noted two things in our discussion so far. The first is that we have given no dates prior to 1000 B.C. That is for the simple reason that archaeologists are not in universal agreement about the chronology of events before the time of David. The second feature is the use of double dating, such as 722/21 B.C. This is because events in ancient time are usually dated in a certain year of some king's reign. So we often cannot be sure within a year as to the exact date.

The two books of *Chronicles* cover a much wider period than the Books of Kings. In fact, the genealogical tables in the first nine chapters go back to Adam (I Chron. 1:1). The historical narrative begins with the death of Saul (c. 10). The rest of I Chronicles is taken up with the reign of David. II Chronicles describes the rule of Solomon and carries us down through the period of the divided kingdom. But the last two verses (II Chron. 36:22-23) give the decree of Cyrus (538 B.C.) for the return of the captives to Judah. It is obvious, then, that Chronicles was not written until after the Babylonian captivity. In fact, it reflects in its opening chapters the greatly increased interest in genealogies that characterizes the postexilic period. To be accepted, the returning captives had to prove their Jewish ancestry. The same feature is prominent in the two following books, Ezra and Nehemiah.

Ezra begins at the point where II Chronicles ends— with the decree of Cyrus (Ezra 1:1-4), which was followed soon (536 B.C.) by the first return from Babylonian captivity under Zerubbabel (c. 2). Ezra's main interest described here is the rebuilding of the Temple (cc. 3—6). The second group returned (458 B.C.) under Ezra himself (cc. 7—8). His primary concern was to restore the true worship of God (cc. 9—10).

The Book of *Nehemiah* is written in the first person, as are parts of Ezra (cc. 8—9). Nehemiah went to Jerusalem (444 B.C.) for the express purpose of rebuilding its walls, which still lay in ruins.

The personalities of these two men are a study in contrasts. When Ezra heard that some of the returned captives were disobeying the Lord's commands, "I rent my garment and my mantle, and plucked off the hair of my head and my beard, and sat down astonied" (Ezra 9:3). When Nehemiah met the same situation, he says: "I contended with them and cursed them, and smote certain of them, and plucked off their hair" (Neh. 13:25). Of course, Nehemiah was the king's appointed governor, while Ezra was a priest and scribe. God could use both of these very different men to do a large work in His kingdom.

The Book of *Esther* belongs to the Persian (postexilic) period, in company with Ezra and Nehemiah. Its purpose was perhaps to explain the origin of the Jewish Feast of Purim (Esther 9:26).

There is no way of knowing just when the Book of *Job* was written. Its setting is "in the land of Uz" (Job 1:1), which probably means the great Syrian desert east and northeast of Palestine. It deals with the timeless, universal problem of human suffering. In literary form it is a majestic drama, discussing the lofty subject of God's dealings with men. As in the case of all devotional classics, its time of writing is unimportant. Along with the Proverbs and Ecclesiastes, it belongs to the "Wisdom Literature" of the Old Testament, which has striking resemblances at some points to the wisdom literature of ancient Egypt and Babylonia.

The *Psalms* were a sort of hymnal for the Israelites. About half the 150 psalms are attributed to David, but most of the others are anonymous. Their dates probably stretch from the time of David to that of the Exile.

The Book of *Proverbs* is stated (1:1; 10:1) as consisting largely of wise sayings written by Solomon. Chapters 25—29 are said to have been copied out by the scribes of Hezekiah some 200 years later (25:1). The last two chapters are attributed respectively to Agur and King Lemuel. It is obvious that Proverbs is a collection of collections of wisdom sayings, gathered over a considerable period of time.

Ecclesiastes (or, "The Preacher") is credited to "the son of David, king in Jerusalem" (1:1). Its main theme is sounded at once: "Vanity of vanities, saith the Preacher, vanity of vanities; all is vanity" (1:2). Such is all life lived "under the sun" (1:3), without reference to God above. "Vanity" literally means emptiness.

The *Song of Solomon,* commonly referred to as Canticles, is also attributed to this king (1:1). In typical Oriental language it describes the joys of marital love. There is a difference of opinion among commentators as to whether or not this is to be taken as an allegory of the relationship between Christ and His bride.

The rest of the Old Testament consists of books of prophecy. The ministry of *Isaiah* is dated from about 740 to 700 B.C. He prophesied in the southern Kingdom of Judah and presumably wrote his matchless book near the close of this period. It should be noted that many scholars argue that chapters 40—66 were written by a Second Isaiah during the Babylonian captivity. But there is no manuscript evidence for this division. The Dead Sea Scroll of Isaiah, discovered in 1947 and dated at about 125 B.C., has the whole book as a unit.

Contemporary with Isaiah was *Hosea* (750-736 B.C.), who prophesied in the northern Kingdom of Israel. He made a dramatic plea to the Lord's wayward wife, Israel, to return to his rightful husband, leaving the false gods. But it was in vain.

Amos may be the earliest of the writing prophets; he is perhaps to be dated around 760 B.C. His emphasis was on social righteousness. He preached in North Israel, especially at Bethel (only 12 miles north of Jerusalem).

The dates for the ministry of *Micah* are the same as those for Isaiah (740-700 B.C.). He too prophesied in the southern Kingdom of Judah. In common with Amos he struck out vigorously against the oppression of the poor.

These are the four prophets of the greatest prophetic age, the eighth century B.C. Some would also include Joel, Obadiah, and Jonah in this period.

Jeremiah prophesied during the last 40 years of the southern Kingdom of Judah (626-586 B.C.). It was his sad task to warn the nation of its impending doom and to see the warning go unheeded. He is called "the weeping prophet" (see 9:1). The Book of *Lamentations* is attributed to him.

Ezekiel was the Lord's prophet to His people in Babylonian captivity. Taken in an early deportation, he apparently ministered 22 years (593-571 B.C.). In common with Isaiah and Jeremiah, Ezekiel not only prophesied to the Judeans, but also to foreign nations. (These are the three longest prophetic books.) He also described a future ideal state of Israel. The book is highly apocalyptic (prophetic).

As in the case of Ezekiel, *Daniel* prophesied in Babylonia (606-536 B.C.). The first six chapters give the history of Daniel, with visions seen by others. The last six chapters describe the visions Daniel saw. The Book of Daniel is the apocalypse of the Old Testament, though there are apocalyptic elements in other books (e.g., Ezekiel).

Hosea, as already noted, was a contemporary of Isaiah. *Joel* (8th or 4th cent.) vividly describes a terrifying plague of locusts. Then he makes a twofold application: to the coming punishment of Judah and to "the day of the Lord." The latter expression is the key phrase of this book.

Amos belongs to the eighth century, as also possibly *Obadiah*. This little book of a single chapter has one theme: the destruction of Edom, to be followed by the restoration of Israel.

According to II Kings 14:25, the prophet *Jonah* ministered during the reign of Jeroboam II of Israel (787-747 B.C.). Told to warn Nineveh of its impending doom, he tried to run away. When Nineveh repented, he complained. The book shows the folly of racial pride, and also God's love for all humanity.

After Micah, "the defender of the poor," comes *Nahum*. He is generally dated between 663 and 612 B.C. He predicted the destruction of Nineveh, which took place in the latter year. Israel's ancient foe, Assyria, was finally punished for her sins when her capital city fell.

Habakkuk prophesied in the same seventh century B.C., near its end (603). He foretold the coming punishment of Judah by the Babylonians. The third chapter of his book is a prayer poem, much like those found in the Book of Psalms.

Zephaniah (about 625 B.C.) blasted out against idolatry in Judah. He pronounced judgment on Judah and foreign nations, but held out hope for the salvation of a remnant.

Haggai and Zechariah both began their ministry at the same time (520 B.C.). The former delivered four messages in that year, all with the same theme: rebuild the Temple. *Zechariah* was also interested in this, as we know from Ezra 6:14. But his prophecies extend from 520 to 518 B.C. A notable feature of his book is the eight visions he saw (1:7—6:15). And like most of the other prophets, he emphasized righteousness rather than ritualism.

Malachi (around 450 B.C.) is the last book of the Old Testament. The name means "my messenger." Looking across the four centuries ahead, he predicted the coming of the Messiah (3:1).

The last 12 books of the Old Testament are called the minor prophets. This is because of their brief size, not because their messages were unimportant.

The New Testament Is Written

a. Paul's Epistles. On their first missionary journey Paul and Barnabas founded several churches in the Roman province of Galatia (in Asia Minor, modern Turkey). Some time later Paul heard that Judaizers had been confusing his new Gentile converts, telling them that they had to be circumcised and keep the law of Moses in order to be saved. Greatly perturbed, the apostle wrote a strong letter to these churches, warning them against falling from the grace of Christ into the pit of legalistic Judaism. If *Galatians* was written about the time of the Council of Jerusalem (A.D. 48), described in the fifteenth chapter of Acts, it is probably the first book of the New Testament to be written. Many scholars would date it a few years later.

On his second missionary journey Paul established a good church in Thessalonica. When he arrived at Corinth he wrote *I Thessalonians,* with its twin emphases on sanctification and the Second Coming. This was in A.D. 50. It has been commonly held that this was the first book of the New Testament. *II Thessalonians* was written just a few months later (A.D. 51), dealing with further problems these people had about the Second Coming.

On his third missionary journey Paul spent three years at Ephesus. While there he wrote *I Corinthians* (A.D. 54 or 55). In it he dealt with three problems he had heard about in the church at Corinth (cc. 1—6), and some six problems about which they had written him (cc. 7—16). These were all practical concerns, but with crucial implications.

After he left Ephesus, Paul wrote *II Corinthians* in Macedonia, probably at Philippi (A.D. 55). Pathetically, he had to defend both his ministry and his own personal integrity in the face of cruel criticism from opponents in Corinth. It was the Corinthian church that gave Paul the most headaches and heartache.

It is of the utmost importance to notice that the first books of the New Testament were not compendiums of systematic theology. Rather, they were missionary letters, written by a missionary to churches he had founded on his missionary journeys. They are "living letters," dealing with life among the people of God.

The busy apostle took time to make a three months' visit to Corinth (Acts 20:3). He wanted to go on west to Rome. But he had been collecting from the Gentile churches an offering for the poor Jewish Christians at Jerusalem.

He felt that he must return to the mother church there, to make sure that this offering was received in a good spirit. Paul's main concern at this point was to weld the Jewish and Gentile churches into one Church of Jesus Christ.

So in lieu of a visit, he wrote a letter to the *Romans* (A.D. 56). In this he gave the fullest exposition he had yet written of the great doctrines of sin, justification, and sanctification. He wanted to make sure that this church in the capital of the Roman Empire was well-established in the central truths of Christianity.

During Paul's two years' imprisonment at Rome (A.D. 59-61), he wrote the four Prison Epistles. *Philemon* is a short personal note to this Christian slave owner about his runaway slave, Onesimus. *Colossians* was sent to the church meeting in this same man's house. It deals with the nature and person of Christ, a crucial question in that part of the world. *Ephesians* was probably a circular letter (in the three oldest Greek manuscripts the words "at Ephesus" are omitted in 1:1), sent first to the mother church at Ephesus, but intended also for the other congregations in the province of Asia. *Philippians* was sent to the church in Macedonia that Paul had founded on his second journey. It is a spontaneous outpouring of joy and thanksgiving. Even in prison Paul kept in touch with his churches.

I Timothy and *Titus* were probably written by Paul about 62-64, soon after he was released from his first Roman imprisonment. Arrested again and placed in a dungeon, the apostle wrote his last letter, *II Timothy*, warning of the apostasy of the last days. These three are called the Pastoral Epistles because they deal with pastoral problems.

b. The General Epistles. Seven letters of the New Testament fall into this category, because they are not addressed to any particular church or individual. Unlike Paul's Epistles, which are named for their destination, these are named after the writer.

James is probably the earliest. Some, in fact, would date it as early as A.D. 45, thus making it the first book of the New Testament to be written. But probably it appeared in the early sixties and *Hebrews* at about the same time (middle sixties) though the latter is not classified as a General Epistle.

I Peter came in the same period, apparently written from Rome. The apostle was seeking to encourage the believers in times of persecution.

The genuineness of *II Peter* has been sharply debated. But assuming the apostle as author, it would have had to be written before A.D. 68, the year of Nero's death. For the Early Church tradition strongly asserts that both Peter and Paul died under Nero. II Peter is apocalyptic in nature.

The three Epistles by John will be reserved for later discussion. *Jude* is much like the second chapter of II Peter.

c. *The Synoptic Gospels and Acts.* The four Gospels are properly placed first in the New Testament, for they give us the foundations of our faith in the life, death, and resurrection of Jesus Christ. But they were not the first books to be written. In fact, John's Gospel was one of the last.

The Gospel of *Mark* was apparently written by John Mark in Rome, either in the late fifties or in 65-70 (as now generally held). *Matthew* appeared a little later, perhaps about A.D. 60, or, as most prefer now, in the seventies. *Luke* was once dated in the early sixties, but is now usually placed at about A.D. 80. Acts appeared either about A.D. 62, as formerly held, or about A.D. 90.

d. *The Johannine Writings.* It is now generally believed that the *Gospel of John,* the three *Epistles of John,* and *Revelation* were all written in the last decade of the first century. We do not know whether the Gospel or the Epistles appeared first. But the Book of Revelation, with its picture of the new heaven and the new earth, forms a perfect capsheaf to the entire divine revelation contained in the Bible.

The Gospel of John was written that its readers might *believe* that Jesus is the Messiah, the Son of God, and that as a result of believing they might have life in Him (20:31). The First Epistle of John was written to believers so that they might *know* that they have eternal life (5:13). The Book of Revelation gives a vision of the glorified Christ in the midst of His Church (c. 1), messages to the seven churches of Asia (cc. 2—3), and a preview of the future (cc. 4—22).

Questions

1. Why is it important that we believe in the divine inspiration of the Bible?

2. In what ways is the Bible a divine-human Book?

3. Why does the Bible give so much space to the history of Israel?

4. What books are included in the "Wisdom Literature" of the Old Testament?

5. What were the earliest books of the New Testament and for what purpose were they written?

6. Why was the Bible written as a Book of life rather than a Book of theology.?

II

Its Preservation

The Bible is actually a Library of 66 books written over a period of some 1,500 years. The 39 books of the Old Testament took about 1,000 years to appear (roughly 1400-400 B.C.). The 27 books of the New Testament were written in a much shorter span of time, about 50 years (A.D. 45-95). Nearly 40 writers were involved in producing these 66 books. How did they finally come to be bound in one volume called "The Bible"?

The word "Bible" come from the Greek plural *ta biblia,* meaning "the books," via the singular Latin term *biblia,* meaning "the book." How did "the Books" become "the Book"? That is the subject of our discussion in this chapter.

The Old Testament Canon

By "canon" we mean an officially accepted list of books. The Protestant canon of the Old Testament is the same as the Hebrew canon accepted by the Jews as constituting "The Holy Scriptures." This is the complete Jewish Bible. The Roman Catholic canon of the Old Testament is longer, including 14 books, or parts of books, that are missing in the Old Testament with which we are familiar. Why this difference?

a. The Hebrew Canon. The basic nucleus of the Hebrew canon is the Torah, or Law of Moses, consisting of the first five books of our Old Testament. The Sadducees of Jesus' day placed primary emphasis on this part of their sacred Scriptures, and even the Pharisees assigned it greater importance. One custom of theirs points this up. In the time of Christ the Scriptures were read in Hebrew in the synagogue services. But most of the Jews of that day did not understand the Hebrew language; they spoke Aramaic. So after reading each verse of the Law in Hebrew, an Aramaic paraphrase was given. In the case of the Prophets, the Aramaic translation came after each three verses. This was evidently being done in a limited way soon after the Babylonian Exile (Neh. 8:8).

In the Hebrew Bible the first book carries the heading *bereshith*, "In the Beginning." It was the custom of the Jews to use the first Hebrew word of each book as the title.

In our Bibles the names of the first five books are taken largely from the Greek Septuagint (to be discussed later). *Genesis* is simply the Greek word for "beginning." *Exodus* is from the Greek *exodos,* meaning "a going out." The main event in this book is the exodus of the Israelites from Egypt. *Leviticus* is so named because it refers largely to the work of the priests, who were Levites. *Numbers* is the English equivalent of the Greek *arithmoi,* its name in the Septuagint. The book records two numberings of the people of Israel, one made at Sinai soon after they left Egypt (c. 1) and the other in the plains of Moab but before they crossed into Canaan (c. 26). *Deuteronomy* is composed of two Greek words, *(Deuteros)* "second," and *nomos,* "law." It describes the second giving of the Law of Moses. The first was to the generation of Israelites that came out of Egypt, and it occurred at Sinai. The second was to the next generation before it entered the Promised Land.

The Hebrew canon contained three divisions: (1) the

Law; (2) the Prophets; (3) the Writings. The Law consisted of the five books of Moses. The Prophets were divided into the Former Prophets and the Latter Prophets, each containing four books. The Former Prophets included Joshua, Judges, Samuel, and Kings (considered as one book each). The Latter Prophets consisted of Isaiah, Jeremiah, Ezekiel and the Twelve. In the Hebrew canon the 12 minor prophets were placed together and referred to as "The Book of the Twelve."

Joshua, Judges, Samuel, and Kings are usually listed by us among the historical books of the Old Testament. But the Jews conceived (rightly) of the history of Israel as prophetic history, and so classified these books under the Prophets.

The third division, the Writings, included the rest of the books of our Old Testament. These were further divided into the three Poetical Books (Psalms, Proverbs, Job), the Five Rolls (Song of Solomon, Ruth, Lamentations, Ecclesiastes, Esther), and the three Historical Books (Daniel, Ezra-Nehemiah, Chronicles).

One passage in the New Testament has a clear reference to this threefold division. In Luke 24:44, Jesus said that all things must be fulfilled "which were written in the law of Moses, and in the prophets, and in the psalms, concerning me." Because the third division, the Writings, began with the Book of Psalms, sometimes the whole group was referred to as "the Psalms."

A quick computation will show that the "books" of the Hebrew canon totaled 24, though this includes all our 39 books. Josephus, the prominent Jewish historian of the first century of the Christian era, speaks of "only twenty-two books" in their sacred Scriptures, probably because there were 22 letters in the Hebrew alphabet. This number was achieved by combining Ruth with Judges and Lamentations with Jeremiah. But finally Ruth and Lamentations were placed with the other short books to form the Five Rolls. II Esdras 14:45 speaks of 24 books.

Perhaps one reason the Five Rolls were put together was their special use in worship. Each would consist of a single scroll. The Song of Solomon was read at the Passover, Ruth at the Feast of Weeks (Pentecost), Ecclesiastes at the Feast of Tabernacles, Esther at the Feast of Purim, and Lamentations on the fast day that commemorated the destruction of Jerusalem in 586 B.C.

In the Hebrew Scriptures today there are 39 books. But the order of the ancient Hebrew canon is preserved, beginning with Genesis and ending with II Chronicles. Isaiah comes after II Kings, and Psalms after Malachi, with Song of Songs following Job, and Daniel following Esther. Thus the threefold division of the Hebrew canon is still the pattern.

When and why did the Jews officially establish their canon of Scripture? The books of the Law had been used from ancient times as possessing divine authority. The individual books of the Prophets were probably accepted as sacred at the time of their appearance. We know that it took some time for all the Writings to be received as Scripture. The Book of Esther was disputed right down to the time of Christ. This may be reflected in the fact that in the Dead Sea caves there have been found fragments of every book of the Old Testament except Esther.

The situation after A.D. 70 called for official action. In that year the Temple was destroyed, along with the city of Jerusalem. This brought an end to the Jewish sacrificial system. The Sadducees, who dominated the priesthood, faded out of sight. The Pharisees, who taught the Scriptures in the numerous synagogues, survived as the leaders. The Jews became the people of the Book. The exact limits of sacred Scripture needed to be set. There must be no doubt as to what books were to be accepted as having divine authority.

There was another very important factor. Christian writings were beginning to appear—the Epistles of Paul, other letters, and especially the Gospels. These must be clearly condemned and excluded from use by adherents of Judaism.

The result was that at the Council of Jamnia, about A.D. 90, the rabbis officially fixed the limits of the Hebrew canon. Included were the 39 books of the present Hebrew Bible, divided into the Law, the Prophets, and the Writings.

b. The Apocrypha. If one happens to come across a large, old pulpit Bible and looks through it, he will discover some rather extensive material between the Old and New Testaments. Actually, he will find there 14 books or parts of books, altogether about five-sixths as long as the New Testament. These are called the Apocrypha.

The term means "hidden." Those who favored these books claimed they were withdrawn from common use because they contained secret wisdom, to be known only by the initiated. Those who rejected them said that they were hidden because they were spurious. Jerome (4th cent.) seems to have been the first to call these books "Apocrypha."

The 14 books are I and II Esdras, Tobit, Judith, Additions to Esther, the Wisdom of Solomon, Ecclesiasticus (also known as the Wisdom of Sirach), Baruch, Susanna, the Song of the Three Children, Bel and the Dragon, the Prayer of Manasseh, and I and II Maccabees. They were apparently written during the three centuries between 200 B.C. and A.D. 100.

In the Greek Septuagint and Latin Vulgate these books are scattered throughout the Old Testament. Martin Luther was the first to separate them. In 1534 he completed his translation of the Bible from the original Greek and Hebrew. Since the apocryphal books were not in the Hebrew Bible, he translated them last and put them by themselves between the Old and New Testaments. Myles Coverdale followed this pattern when he put out the first printed English Bible the next year, 1535. All the Protestant English Bibles did the same, down to and including the King James Version (1611). The Catholic Bibles in English still have the Apocrypha scattered throughout the Old Testament, as in the Latin Vulgate.

But the Bibles with which we are most familiar today do not have the apocryphal books in them at all. If they were in the original King James Version, how and when did they get out?

The Great Bible of 1539 in its prologue quotes the statement of Jerome that these books were good for edifying, but not authoritative. The Geneva Bible of 1560 went a little further, saying that they were not to be used for deciding doctrine, but for knowledge of history and instruction in godly living. But the Bishops' Bible (1568) issued no such warning. Since the King James Version (1611) was a revision of the Bishops' Bible, it simply gave them the heading "Apocrypha," without any disparaging note. In fact, one of the men who produced the King James Version became Archbishop of Canterbury and issued a decree that anyone who published the English Bible without the Apocrypha should be imprisoned for a year!

But the Puritans "persecuted the Apocrypha," as Frederick Kenyon aptly observes. As far back as 1590 some copies of their Geneva Bible began to appear without the apocryphal books. By 1629 the same thing was happening to the King James Version, under Puritan influence.

The official view of the Church of England is stated in its Thirty-nine Articles. After speaking of the "canonical books" it goes on to say; "And the other Books (as Jerome saith) the Church doth read for example of life and instruction of manners; but yet doth it not apply them to establish any doctrine."

It was in the early nineteenth century that action was finally taken to exclude the apocryphal books. The National

Bible Society of Scotland took the position that, if these books were not the inspired Word of God, money should not be wasted in printing them as part of the Bible. It petitioned the British and Foreign Bible Society, which voted in 1827 not to use any of its funds in publishing the Apocrypha. From that time most copies of the King James Version omitted these books.

The English Revised Version came out in 1885 without the Apocrypha, but did publish the latter in 1894. Similarly, the Revised Standard Version appeared in 1952 with no Apocrypha. But at the request of the General Convention of the Protestant Episcopal church in that year, it finally made up for the deficiency by putting out a translation of the Apocrypha in 1965. Meanwhile Professor Edgar J. Goodspeed of the University of Chicago had popularized the Apocrypha among many Protestants by having his excellent translation of it included in *An American Translation: The Complete Bible* (1939). The *New English Bible: New Testament* came out in 1961, but that version appeared in its complete form, with the Apocrypha, in 1970. One might say that the Apocrypha is "in" again, at least for some Protestants.

What should be our attitude toward the Apocrypha? In the first place, we must recognize that there is much material here of historical and religious value. But we agree with the sound Protestant opinion of the last 400 years that these books are not a part of the inspired, authoritative Word of God. We feel that as such they have no place in the Bible, but should be studied separately.

Since most Protestants are not familiar with the Apocrypha, a brief characterization of each book may be in order. And since the Roman Catholic church officially holds these books to be a part of the inspired, authoritative Bible, we need to know what their nature is.

I Esdras (about 150 B.C.) tells of the restoration of the Jews to Palestine after the Babylonian exile. It draws considerably from Chronicles, Ezra, and Nehemiah, but the author has added much legendary material.

The most interesting item is the Story of the Three Guardsmen. They were debating what was the strongest thing in the world. One said, "Wine"; another, "the King"; the third, "Woman and Truth." They put these three answers under the king's pillow. When he awoke he required the three men to defend their answers. The unanimous decision was: "Truth is greatly and supremely strong." Because Zerubbabel had given this answer he was allowed, as a reward, to rebuild the Temple at Jerusalem.

II Esdras (A.D. 100) is an apocalyptic work, containing seven visions. Martin Luther was so confused by these visions that he is said to have thrown the book into the Elbe River.

Tobit (early 2nd cent. B.C.) is a short novel. Strongly Pharisaic in tone, it emphasizes the Law, clean foods, ceremonial washings, charity, fasting and prayer. It is clearly unscriptural in its statement that almsgiving atones for sin.

Judith (about the middle of 2nd cent. B.C.) is also fictitious and Pharisaic. The heroine of this novel is Judith, a beautiful Jewish widow. When her city was beseiged she took her maid, together with Jewish clean food, and went out to the tent of the attacking general. He was enamored of her beauty and gave her a place in his tent. Fortunately, he had imbibed too freely and sank into a drunken stupor. Judith took his sword and cut off his head. Then she and her maid left the camp, taking his head in their provision bag. It was hung on the wall of a nearby city and the leaderless Assyrian army was defeated.

Additions to Esther (about 100 B.C.). Esther stands alone among the books of the Old Testament in having no mention of God. We are told that Esther and Mordecai fasted but not specifically that they prayed. To compensate for this lack, the Additions have long prayers attributed to these two, together with a couple of letters supposedly written by Artaxerxes.

The Wisdom of Solomon (about A.D. 40) was written to keep the Jews from falling into skepticism, materialism, and idolatry. As in Proverbs, Wisdom is personified. There are many noble sentiments expressed in this book.

Ecclesiasticus, or Wisdom of Sirach (about 180 B.C.), shows a high level of religious wisdom, somewhat like the canonical Book of Proverbs. It also contains much practical advice. For instance, on the subject of after-dinner speeches it says (32:8):

"Speak concisely; say much in few words;

Act like a man who knows more than he says."

And again (33:4):

"Prepare what you have to say,

And then you will be listened to."

In his sermons John Wesley quotes several times from the Book of Ecclesiasticus. It is still widely used in Anglican circles.

Baruch (about A.D. 100) represents itself as being written by Baruch, the scribe of Jeremiah, in 582 B.C. Actually, it is probably trying to interpret the destruction of Jerusalem in A.D. 70. The book urges the Jews not to revolt again, but to be in submission to the emperor. In spite of this the Bar-Cochba revolution against Roman rule took place soon after, in A.D. 132-35. The sixth chapter of Baruch contains the so-called "Letter of Jeremiah," with its strong warning against idolatry—probably addressed to Jews in Alexandria, Egypt.

Our Book of Daniel contains 12 chapters. In the first century before Christ a thirteenth chapter was added, the story of *Susanna*. She was the beautiful wife of a leading Jew in Babylon, to whose house the Jewish elders and judges frequently came. Two of these became enamored of her and tried to seduce her. When she cried out, the two elders said they had found her in the arms of a young man. She was brought to trial. Since there were two witnesses who agreed in their testimony, she was convicted and sentenced to death.

But a young man named Daniel interrupted the proceedings and began to cross-examine the witnesses. He asked each one separately under which tree in the garden they had found Susanna with a lover. When they gave different answers they were put to death and Susanna was saved.

Bel and the Dragon was added at about the same time and called chapter 14 of Daniel. Its main purpose was to show the folly of idolatry. It really contains two stories.

In the first, King Cyrus asked Daniel why he did not worship Bel, since that deity showed his greatness by daily consuming many sheep, together with much flour and oil. So Daniel scattered ashes on the floor of the Temple where the food had been placed that evening. In the morning the king took Daniel in to show him that Bel had eaten all the food during the night. But Daniel showed the king in the ashes on the floor the footprints of the priests and their families who had entered secretly under the table. The priests were slain and the temple destroyed.

The story of the Dragon is just as obviously legendary in character. Along with Tobit, Judith, and Susanna, these stories may be classified as purely Jewish fiction. They have little if any religious value.

The *Song of the Three Hebrew Children* follows Dan. 3:23 in the Septuagint and the Vulgate. Borrowing heavily from Psalms 148, it is antiphonal like Psalms 136, having 32 times the refrain: "Sing praise to him and greatly exalt him forever."

The *Prayer of Manasseh* was composed in Maccabean times (2nd cent. B.C.) as the supposed prayer of Manasseh, the wicked king of Judah. It was obviously suggested by the statement in II Chron, 33:19—"His prayer also, and how God was entreated of him . . . behold, they are written among the sayings of the seers." Since this prayer is not found in the Bible, some scribe had to make up the deficiency!

I Maccabees (1st cent. B.C.) is perhaps the most valuable book in the Apocrypha. For it describes the exploits of the three Maccabean brothers—Judas, Jonathan, and Simon. Along with Josephus it is our most important source for the history of this crucial and exciting period in Jewish history.

II Maccabees (same time) is not a sequel to I Maccabees, but a parallel account, treating only the victories of Judas Maccabaeus. It is generally thought to be more legendary than I Maccabees.

The New Testament Canon

At about A.D. 140 in Rome a heretic named Marcion adopted as his New Testament 10 Epistles of Paul (excluding the Pastorals) and a mutilated Gospel of Luke (first two chapters missing). He also rejected the entire Old Testament. To counteract his influence, it was necessary for the orthodox Christian Church to think about fixing the limits of its canon.

At the other extreme from Marcion, many churches in the East (for example, Alexandria, Egypt) were reading in their public services certain books of the New Testament Apocrypha. A fifth-century manuscript, Alexandrinus, has the First Epistle of Clement of Rome attached to it. The Epistle of Barnabas and the Shepherd of Hermas (both 2nd-cent. books) are found at the end of Sinaiticus, a fourth-century manuscript. Clearly a decision needed to be made as to exactly what books were to be included in the canon.

A third factor was the edict of Diocletian, in A.D. 303, demanding the destruction of all sacred books of Christianity. Would a Christian want to risk his life by having in his possession a religious book that was not really inspired by God?

It is usually thought that the only genuine Christian writing we have from the first century, outside the New

Testament, is Clement of Rome's First Epistle, written about A.D. 95. It contains references to Matthew, Romans, and I Corinthians, and many allusions to Hebrews.

The earliest church fathers of the second century, such as Ignatius and Polycarp, show a wide acquaintance with Paul's Epistles, some of the Gospels, and I Peter and I John. This use of our New Testament books increased steadily down through the middle of that century. For instance, Justin Martyr (A.D. 150) shows a knowledge of the four Gospels, Acts, several of Paul's Epistles, Hebrews, I Peter, and Revelation. By the end of the second century it is clear that Irenaeus in Gaul (France), Clement of Alexandria (Egypt), and Tertullian of Carthage (North Africa) all had essentially the same New Testament as we have today.

During the third century there was considerable dispute about the canonicity of seven of our New Testament books. These were Hebrews, James, II Peter, II and III John, Jude, and Revelation. This uncertainty continued on into the fourth century. The first exact list of our 27 books is found in the Easter letter of Athanasius, in A.D. 367. Finally, nearly the close of the fourth century, in A.D. 397, the Council of Carthage decreed that only "canonical" books should be read in the churches. It then proceeded to list exactly the 27 books of our New Testament. From that day to this the canon of the New Testament has remained the same for the Roman Catholic church and has been the Protestant canon since the Reformation. We believe the Holy Spirit led in the selections made.

Questions

1. What is the advantage of having the Bible written by many different men rather than by one man (cf. Eph. 3: 18)?

2. In what ways is the Bible a Library of books and in what way is it "the Book"?

3. What were the three divisions of the Hebrew canon, and which books were included in each division?

4. What is the difference between the Catholic and Protestant Old Testaments, and what is the reason for this?

5. Why did the Early Church form a canon of the New Testament?

6. When was the canon finalized officially?

III

Its Transmission

We do not have the original copy of a single book of the Bible. This one fact alone demands a careful investigation of the text of both the Old and New Testaments. Are we justified in believing that we have a reliably authentic copy of each of the 66 books of the sacred canon?

The Old Testament Text

We are fortunate to have the privilege of living in the age of archaeological discoveries. The time was when some scholars asserted that Moses could not have written the Pentateuch because the art of writing was unknown at that early date (about 1400 B.C.). But, as in many other cases, archaeology has silenced this argument forever. At Ur and Nippur, in Messopotamia, thousands of clay tablets have been dug up, going back as far as 2100 B.C. That is, we have tablets from Abraham's old hometown that were inscribed at the very time he lived there—half a millennium before Moses' day. From the other great center of earliest civilization, the Nile valley, have come papyrus manuscripts from before 2000 B.C. Some of them contain texts which claim to have been written originally before 3000 B.C. It is evident that writing is an ancient art.

In 1929 a startling discovery was made at the site of

the ancient city of Ugarit, on the northwest coast of Syria. Archaeological excavations revealed a large building, which housed a library, a scribes' school, and the home of the chief priest of the local cult. In the library were found hundreds of tablets written in a strange script. Later excavations (1952-53) unearthed the ancient Ugaritic alphabet, composed of 30 letters. The tablet on which it is written is thought to come from the fourteenth century B.C., near the time of Moses. The Ugaritic language is Semitic, and so a sister language to Hebrew. In his recent (1966, 1968) two-volume commentary on the Psalms in "The Anchor Bible," Dahood has made considerable use of parallels in Ugaritic literature as a help in understanding the meaning of Hebrew terms.

Moses was "learned in all the wisdom of the Egyptians" (Acts 7:22), having received a royal education in the literature of ancient Egypt. Also when the Israelites under Joshua entered the land of Canaan, they found an alphabet and a large body of religious literature in a Semitic language. So the physical tools were at hand for writing the Old Testament.

As to writing materials, the Egyptians used leather scrolls at an early time. Specimens from about 2000 B.C. have been discovered. The later Jewish Talmud required that all copies of the Law should be written on skins and in roll form. This rule is still in force.

a. The Pre-Massoretic Text. Humanly speaking, it is impossible for anyone to copy by hand a document as long as the prophecy of Isaiah without making some mistakes. And we must remember that all the copies of the books of the Old and New Testaments were made by hand until the middle of the fifteenth century (A.D. 1456). That means that some had been copied for nearly 3,000 years and all of them for well over 1,000 years. Not until the modern age of printing was it possible to produce large numbers of copies of a book, all of them exactly the same.

So it is not surprising to find some differences in the text of the Old Testament manuscripts. We may be thankful, however, for the fact that the Hebrew scribes were very careful in their copying of the sacred Scriptures. They realized that this was a serious responsibility. R. K. Harrison says: "In the immediate pre-Christian period the Jewish authorities gave a great deal of thought to the preservation of the Old Testament text in as pure a form as possible, a concern prompted as much by the existence of manuscript variants as by differences between the Hebrew and LXX texts."[1] That is, they tried to correct errors that had crept into the text through centuries of copying manuscripts from one generation to another.

In the second century of the Christian era Rabbi Aqiba sought to fix the text with exactness. He is credited with saying that "the accurate transmission *(massoreth)* of the text is a fence for the Torah."[2] For the purpose of closer study, the scribes divided the Hebrew text into verses.

b. The Massoretic Text. Around the beginning of the sixth century the work of the scribes in copying the Old Testament manuscripts was taken over by the Massoretes, who functioned about A.D. 500-1000. They worked with meticulous care. For each book of the Old Testament they counted the number of verses, words, and even letters. They went so far as to identify the middle letter of each book! By counting all the letters they could make sure that not one had been added or left out. This meant that the text was now copied with greater accuracy than ever before.

But the contribution for which the Massoretes are most famous is the addition of vowel points. The Hebrew alphabet consists of consonants only. It is as if we were to write the

---

[1] *Introduction to the Old Testament* (Grand Rapids, Mich.: Wm. B. Eerdmans Publishing Co., 1969), p. 211.
[2] *Ibid.*

first verse of Genesis as follows (in Hebrew the articles and prepositions are attached to the nouns):

NTHBGNNNGGDCRTDTHHVNNDTHRTH

It is obvious that a combination of three consonants—the most frequent number for a Hebrew root—could yield several different words, depending on what vowels were inserted between the consonants. As an example, in English, *l-v-d* could be *lived*, *loved*, or *livid*. Of course, the context would usually, but not always, indicate which of these it would be.

There is an important factor to be taken into consideration, however. It appears that all reading in ancient times was done aloud. In any case, the Scriptures were read aloud each Sabbath in the synagogues, and earlier in the Temple and Tabernacle. Also the scribes read the Word of God aloud each day. At that time the method of instruction in the schoolroom was for the teacher to read a sentence from a scroll and then for his pupils to repeat it after him. In this way the people were familiar with the sound as well as the sense.

But across the centuries it was inevitable that there would arise some differences of opinion as to how specific words should be pronounced. Also scribes would make mistakes in copying the consonants. What was really the traditional text?

The Massoretes—from *massora*, "tradition"—undertook the important task of correcting the text and standardizing it. To ensure accuracy of pronunciation it was necessary to indicate in some way the vowel sounds. So to the consonantal text, which had been copied for hundreds of years, the Massoretes added "vowel points"—combinations of dots and lines under the consonants (in one case above the consonant) The resulting text is called the Massoretic Text, and this is the standard text of the Hebrew Old Testament studied today. With the extreme care the Massoretes gave to the copying of the Scriptures, this text has come down to us from the Middle Ages with little change. And since the fifteenth century it has been fixed solidly in print.

c. *The Dead Sea Scrolls.* Still, the oldest Hebrew manuscript we had was from about the beginning of the tenth century (A.D. 900). How would we know that this represented the Hebrew text in use in the days of Christ, to say nothing of Old Testament times? There seemed to be no certain answer that could be given to this disturbing question.

As has so often happened in the past hundred years of archaeological research, the answer finally came. In 1947 a complete manuscript of the Hebrew text of Isaiah was found. Paleographers date it about 125 B.C. So it is 1,000 years older than the oldest copy of Isaiah known up to that time.

The story of this discovery is one of the most fascinating tales of modern times. In February or March of 1947 a Bedouin shepherd boy named Muhammad was searching for a lost goat. He tossed a stone into a hole in a cliff on the west side of the Dead Sea, about eight miles south of Jericho. To his surprise, he heard the sound of shattering pottery. Investigating, he discovered an amazing sight. On the floor of the cave were several large jars containing leather scrolls, wrapped in linen cloth. Because the jars were carefully sealed, the scrolls had been preserved in excellent condition for nearly 1,900 years. (They were evidently placed there in A.D. 68.)

Five of the scrolls found in Dead Sea Cave I, as it is now called, were bought by the archbishop of the Syrian Orthodox Monastery at Jerusalem. Meanwhile, three other scrolls were purchased by Professor Sukenik of the Hebrew University there. Later the archbishop brought his five scrolls to the United States, where agents negotiated the purchase of them by the state of Israel for $250,000. So now, all eight scrolls from the first cave are on display in Jerusalem. They can be seen in what is called "The Shrine of the Book," a cave-like building specially constructed to house them.

When the scrolls were first discovered, no publicity was given to them. In November of 1947, two days after Professor Sukenik purchased three scrolls and two jars from the cave, he wrote in his diary: "It may be that this is one of the greatest finds ever made in Palestine, a find we never so much as hoped for." But these significant words were not published at the time.

Fortunately, in February of 1948, the archbishop, who could not read Hebrew, phoned the American School of Oriental Research in Jerusalem and told about the scrolls. By good providence, the acting director of the school at the moment was a young scholar named John Trever, who was also an excellent amateur photographer. With arduous, dedicated labor he photographed each column of the great Isaiah scroll, which is 24 feet long and 10 inches high. He developed the plates himself and sent a few prints by airmail to Dr. W. F. Albright of Johns Hopkins University, who was widely recognized as the dean of American biblical archaeologists. By return airmail Albright wrote: "My heartiest congratulations on the greatest manuscript discovery of modern times! . . . What an absolutely incredible find! And there can happily not be the slightest doubt in the world about the genuineness of the manuscript." He dated it about 100 B.C.

Among the other manuscripts found in Cave I were a commentary on Habakkuk and a "Rule of the Community," a sort of manual or discipline for the religious community. In 1950-51 the American Schools of Oriental Research published these two, together with the Isaiah scroll. In 1954 the Hebrew University published three other manuscripts from Cave I, including an interesting document called "The War Between the Children of Light and the Children of

Darkness." This terminology reminds us of John's Gospel and First Epistle.

Archaeologists have investigated a total of 14 caves on the west side of the Dead Sea. Besides Cave I, the most valuable finds were in Caves IV and XI. Cave IV yielded tens of thousands of fragments, including parts of every Old Testament book except Esther. Fragments of the Apocrypha were also found. The favorite biblical books of the community were Genesis, Deuteronomy, the Psalms, and Isaiah. These are doubtless the very four that would be chosen from the Old Testament by a thoughtful Christian today.

Near these caves archaeologists uncovered the ruins of an ancient fortified monastery. One can now go through this building and see the various rooms. The most exciting is the Scriptorium, where the scribes copied the manuscripts. Here were found a long, narrow table, a bench, and two inkwells. There was also an assembly hall, about 75 by 15 feet in size. The walls of the monastery enclosed a pottery—where the cave jars were probably made—a forge, a grain mill, a bakery, and a laundry.

The place is known today as Qumran. It is generally agreed that the Qumran community belonged to a Jewish sect called the Essenes. In A.D. 68, two years before the destruction of Jerusalem, the Roman army burned the monastery. As the enemy approached, the Essene scribes apparently hid their valuable manuscripts in the nearby caves, so that they would not be found and destoyed. Today we can be thankful that they took this precaution.

The biblical scrolls found at Qumran have been dated from 200 B.C. to A.D. 68. The Isaiah scroll, as we have seen, is dated about 125 B.C., a thousand years earlier than the oldest previously known manuscript of that book.

The crucial question that immediately comes to mind is this: How does its text compare with the Massoretic text from the Middle Ages? The answer is reassuring. It agrees closely with it. As would be expected, there are minor variations. About 14 of these variant readings were accepted by the translators of the Revised Standard Version (1952). They are identified by footnotes saying, "One ancient MS." In the case of other manuscripts, especially from Cave IV, it has been found that in the historical books of the Old Testament the Qumran text is often closer to the Septuagint than to the Massoretic text. Scholars now have new tools for establishing a more exact text of the Old Testament.

The New Testament Text

"There are thousands of variant readings in the Greek New Testament." That statement, found some years ago in a popular magazine, is technically true. But the impression given by it in the context of the article was morally untrue. For the author probably left most of his readers somewhat shattered with the feeling that the Greek text of the New Testament must be in a state of utter chaos.

Such, of course, is not the case at all. The vast majority of these variations are in the realm of differences in spelling or grammatical form, matters that have no significance whatever for the meaning of the text.

In 1853 two great Cambridge scholars, B. F. Westcott and F. J. A. Hort, set out to construct an accurate text of the New Testament based on the best Greek manuscripts. After over 20 years of arduous, devoted work, they published the fruit of their labors in *The New Testament in the Original Greek* (1881)—a standard work used by generations of students of the Greek New Testament.

Not so well known is Volume II, "Introduction and Appendix," actually written by Hort. In it he says of the Greek text of the New Testament: "The proportion of words virtually accepted on all hands as raised above doubt is very great, not less, on a rough computation, than seven eights of the whole." He goes on to say that, "setting aside differences of orthography (spelling, etc.), the words in our opinion still subject to doubt only make up about one sixtieth of the whole New Testament." He then asserts that ". . . the amount of what can in any sense be called substantial variation is but a small fraction of the whole residuary variation, and can hardly form more than a thousandth part of the entire text."[3]

Most scholars today would agree that Hort's last statement is a bit too optimistic. Nevertheless, it underscores the fact of the basic reliability of the Greek text of the New Testament as we now have it.

a. Kinds of Error. No two manuscripts of the Greek New Testament are exactly alike. Humanly speaking, this is unavoidable. It would be well-nigh impossible for two people to copy by hand the entire Greek text of the New Testament without making any mistakes. And the books of the New Testament were all copied by hand for over 1,000 years before the age of printing began in the middle of the fifteenth century.

There are two main classes of unintentional mistakes made by copyists. These are errors of the eye and errors of the ear.

(1) *Errors of the eye.* Such mistakes will almost inevitably be made by anyone who copies a long document. But the problem is compounded in the case of the Greek New Testament by several factors.

To begin with, in the older Greek manuscripts there are not only no chapter and verse divisions and no separation into sentences, but not even any separation between words. It is as if we should write the first verse of Luke's Gospel as follows:

[3]B. F. Westcott and F. J. A. Hort, *The New Testament in the Original Greek* (New York: Harper and Brothers, 1882), II, 2.

FORASMUCHASMANYHAVETAKENINHAN
DTOSETFORTHINORDERADECLARATION
OFTHOSETHINGSWHICHAREMOSTS
URELYBELIEVEDAMONGUS

And so it goes on, line after line, column after column, through a whole book of the New Testament. When a person was copying one manuscript from another, he might make a wrong division between words. Of course, he would usually be aware of this and correct the mistake. But ISAWABUNDANCEONTHETABLE could be taken as "I saw a bun dance on the table" or "I saw abundance on the table." Mistakes of this type are found in later Greek manuscripts (e.g., 15th cent.), when separation between words was introduced.

In the second place, the oldest Greek manuscripts commonly use abbreviations for such words as God, Christ, Jesus, and Son, with an overhead line connecting the first and last letters. Christ appears as *XC*, Jesus as *IC*, Son as *YC*, each with a line overhead. It is obvious that it would be easier to confuse these abbreviations than it would be if the words were written out in full.

A third type of error is still very common today—the omission of a line when two consecutive lines begin or end with the same word. One who is frequently preparing copy for a typist soon learns to avoid setting this trap! A similar type of situation is the omission or addition of similar clauses, or even sentences.

(2) *Errors of the ear.* As we have seen, errors of the eye would be made by a scribe who was copying one manuscript from another. But sometimes a man would sit at a table, slowly reading aloud a manuscript to a group of scribes seated in front of him. This was the only kind of publishing house in those days, and usually not more than 40 scribes would be involved at a time—a very different situation

from a modern printing plant, which can turn out thousands of identical copies of a book.

In the case of a group copying from dictation, errors of the ear were bound to occur. This would happen today in such copying of English manuscripts. For there are many words that sound alike but differ in spelling and meaning. One scribe would hear it one way; another would take it a different way.

Again, to compound the situation, most of the vowels and dipthongs in the Greek of that day, as in modern Greek, were pronounced practically alike, sounding like our long *e*. I once sat in a Greek prayer meeting in Athens, where I would not have been able to follow the Scripture reading at all if I had not held a Greek Testament in my hand. In a Greek-speaking Church of the Nazarene in Sydney, Australia, I had a similar experience. When I got up to preach I announced: "Now I'm going to read the pastor's scripture lesson the way *we* pronounce it." I proceeded to do so, much to the enjoyment of the audience!

b. Abundance of Manuscripts. Lest the reader feel unduly disturbed by the picture we have just painted, let us hasten to say that most of these errors can be quickly spotted and eliminated in constructing a Greek text of the New Testament today. We now have over 5,000 manuscripts of the Greek New Testament, in whole or in part. By carefully comparing them we can readily weed out most of the mistakes made in copying. In cases where we cannot be absolutely certain what was the exact original text of the New Testament—and there are such—we can be comforted with the assurance that not one of these variant readings adversely affects a single doctrine of our Christian faith.

(1) *Papyri.* The common writing material of the first century was papyrus, from which we get our term "paper." It was made by taking stalks of the papyrus plant and slic-

ing the pith into thin strips. Two layers of these strips were placed together crosswise, with a kind of glue between, and allowed to dry. Obviously the resulting material was brittle and fragile. It is usually assumed that all the New Testament was written on papyrus, with the possible exception of the four Gospels and Acts, and that is the basic reason that no original copies have survived.

Papyri were unknown in modern times until 1778, when some fellahin, digging in the Fayum district of southern Egypt, happened across an earthenware pot containing about 50 papyrus rolls.

But the first major discovery of Greek papyri took place in 1897. Two Britishers, Grenfell and Hunt, were excavating near the village of Oxyrhynchus, about 120 miles south of Cairo. In the rubbish mounds of the town they came across many bushels of papyrus material, most of it consisting of secular papers and documents. Significant new light was thrown on the meaning of many New Testament words by the study of these contemporary papyri.

A good example of this may be seen in the repeated statement of Jesus, "They have their reward" (Matt. 6: 2, 5, 16). The regular Greek word for "have" in the New Testament is *echo*. But here we find the compound *apecho*. The rubbish heaps of Egypt disclosed hundreds of formal receipts, all of them having this word. So modern translations have the more adequate rendering, "They have received their reward." The meaning of Jesus' words is that those who practice their religion in order to get the praise of men virtually give a receipt, "Paid in full." They can claim no further reward in the next life. We have to decide whether eternal dividends are worth sacrificing on the altar of earthly glory.

Papyrus manuscripts of the Greek New Testament are a more recent discovery. The largest and most important of them have come to light since 1930. The Chester Beatty Papyri (Dublin, Ireland) include three documents from the third century—one of the four Gospels and Acts, very incomplete; another of the Pauline Epistles, nearly complete; and a third of Revelation, the middle part. These are numbered Papyrus 45, 46, and 47. Since then, the outstanding manuscripts have been the Bodmer Papyri (Geneva, Switzerland), discovered and edited in the 1950's and 1960's. Papyrus 66 of John's Gospel is thought to have come from around A.D. 200, only about a hundred years after the Gospel was originally written. Papyrus 72 has the earliest known text of Jude, I Peter, and II Peter. This is also from the third century. Another important manuscript from the third century is Papyrus 75, containing much of the Gospels of Luke and John.

Only about 80 New Testament papyrus manuscripts have been found to date. But they are of great importance, since they reach back to the third century.

(2) *Uncials.* There are about 270 uncial manuscripts extant, reaching from the fourth to ninth centuries. These are written in large block letters and are second in importance only to the papyri.

We have two great uncial Bibles from the fourth century, Vaticanus and Sinaiticus. The former, as the name suggests, is in the Vatican Library at Rome. The second derives its name from the fact that it was found on Mount Sinai. Today it can be seen in the British Museum in London. The last part of the New Testament section of Vaticanus is broken off and lost, but Sinaiticus has a complete New Testament.

The story of the discovery of the Sinaitic manuscript may serve to show something of the labor expended in seeking to recover the oldest Greek text. In 1844, Constantine Tischendorf made a trip to the Middle East in search of ancient manuscripts. One day he was working the library of the monastery of St. Catherine at Mount Sinai, reputed to be the oldest Christian monastery in the world. Noticing some stray leather pages of a manuscript lying in a waste-basket, he took a look at them. To his astonishment, he found that they were leaves of the oldest Greek Bible he had ever seen. He rescued 43 of these leaves, which the monks let him have. They told him they had already burned the contents of two baskets! After extracting a promise from them that they would not destroy any more, he took the 43 leaves with him back to Leipzig. Returning to the monastery in 1853, he looked in vain for the rest of the manuscript. The monks would tell him nothing.

In 1859 he decided to make another attempt, sponsored by the czar of Russia, the patron of the Greek Orthodox church. After some fruitless days at the monastery of St. Catherine, he gave orders to his camel drivers to be ready to leave for Cairo the next morning.

That evening the steward of the monastery invited Tischendorf to his room to see an old copy of the Septuagint. Soon the German scholar held in his hands a heap of loose leaves wrapped in a red cloth. To his astonishment, he discovered that it was the very manuscript from which had come the 43 leaves he had acquired 15 years earlier. At last his eager search had been rewarded.

Covering his feelings of extreme joy, Tischendorf casually asked if he might take the manuscript to his room to examine it further. There he stayed up all night, copying part of it, since he had no assurance that he could take it with him.

In the morning he tried in vain to purchase it. Then he asked for permission to take it to Cairo to study, but the monk in charge of the library objected. When he got to Cairo, however, he persuaded the superior of the monastery there to send to Sinai for the manuscript. Tischendorf was allowed to copy it a few sheets at a time.

Just then an ecclesiastical situation provided the necessary opportunity for getting the prize. A new archbishop was to be elected. The monks had their candidate whom they wanted chosen. Tischendorf suggested that they present the precious manuscript to the czar of Russia, the protector of the Greek church, to gain his support for their candidate. And so it was done. In addition to a favorable election, the monks received a present of money from the czar, while the manuscript was safely deposited in St. Petersburg.

In 1933 the Soviet government of Russia, caring little for a Bible but needing cash, offered to sell Codex Sinaiticus. It was purchased by the British Museum for half a million dollars, the highest price ever paid for a book up to that time.

In the United States, the oldest Greek manuscript of the four Gospels is Washingtoniensis (W), so called because it is in the Smithsonian Institution in Washington. It comes from the late fourth or early fifth century. There are several other important uncials from the fifth century (A, C, D), but most of the uncials came from later centuries.

(3) *Minuscules*. From the ninth century to the fifteenth—when printing began—we have over 2,750 minuscule or cursive manuscripts, so called because they are written in a small running script. They contain the medieval Greek text of the New Testament, which is late and inferior.

With such an abundance of manuscript materials at our disposal we can rest assured that we have ample means for arriving at a very close approximation of the original Greek text of the New Testament.

Questions

1. What do we mean by the Massoretic text of the Old Testament?

2. When were the Dead Sea Scrolls discovered, and what is their value for Old Testament studies?

3. What is the reason why there are variant readings in Greek manuscripts of the New Testament?

4. What is the difference between errors of the eye and errors of the ear?

5. What is the importance of textual criticism of the New Testament?

6. Why may we feel confident that we have a reliable Greek text of the New Testament?

IV

Its Translation

Aramaic Targums

After the Babylonian captivity there were many Jews who could not understand the Hebrew Scriptures. So Aramaic Targums, or paraphrases, were added when the Law and the Prophets were read in the synagogues. This custom may have begun as early as the time of Ezra (Neh. 8:8).

At first these were simple oral paraphrases. As time went by they became more elaborate, taking on the nature of explanations and even theological interpretations. Gradually they became fixed in form and were finally reduced to writing during the Christian era. Originating in Palestine, many of them were edited in Babylonia in the early Middle Ages.

Soon after the time of Christ the Samaritan Pentateuch (Hebrew written in Samaritan characters) was translated into the Aramaic dialect used by the Samaritans. This is called the Samaritan Targum.

Greek Versions

It may be well to define the word "version" before proceeding further. A version means a translation. Since the Old Testament was written in Hebrew we cannot speak of a Hebrew version of the Old Testament. Similarly, we cannot talk about a Greek version of the New Testament. But we can speak of a Greek version of the Old Testament or a Latin version of the New Testament.

   a. The Septuagint. The earliest translation of the Hebrew Bible (our Old Testament) is called the Septuagint, the Latin word for "seventy." This name is due to a false tradition, based on the so-called Letter of Aristeas, that there were about 70 translators.

   This letter claims to be written by an official in the court of Ptolemy Philadelphus, ruler of Egypt (285-247 B.C.). It tells how the emperor wanted to have in the royal library at Alexandria a copy of all the books of that day. So he sent a request to the high priest in Jerusalem, asking for 72 capable men (six from each tribe) to translate the Law of Moses into Greek. After a royal welcome at the Alexandrian court, the 72 men worked on an island in seclusion, completing the translation in 72 days.

   This legendary account was later exaggerated further. Philo, the great Jewish philosopher at Alexandria (30 B.C.-A.D. 45), said that the translators worked independently. When each had finished the complete translation, the 72 results were identical. Anyone familiar at all with translation work knows that this is utterly preposterous. A later writer, Epiphanius, even claimed that the entire Old Testament (including the Apocrypha) was all done at that time. As we have seen, the apocryphal books were all written at a later date.

   What, then, are the facts? It is generally agreed that the five books of Moses were translated around the middle of the third century B.C. and that the rest of the Old Testament was rendered into Greek during the following hundred years (250-150 B.C.). Strictly speaking, the term Septuagint should be applied only to the Greek translation of the Pentateuch. But for centuries it has been applied to the whole Greek Old Testament, and so we follow that custom.

We have already noted that the Hebrew alphabet has only consonants. Consequently the Hebrew text of the Old Testament is shorter than the Greek translation, since the Greek alphabet includes vowels. As a result, the Books of Samuel, Kings, and Chronicles were each found too long to go on a single scroll. In the Septuagint, therefore, they were divided into I and II Samuel, I and II Kings, I and II Chronicles, as we have them today in our Bibles. However, in the Septuagint, I and II Samuel became I and II Kings, while our I and II Kings became III and IV Kings. This was carried over into the Latin Vulgate and so into Catholic English Bibles.

Since a majority of Old Testament quotations in the New Testament are from the Septuagint, this version has great significance for us. And in addition to actual quotation, much of the terminology of the Greek New Testament has its basis in the Septuagint.

The fifteenth century was an outstanding one in history. It was in 1492 that Columbus discovered America and opened up the New World of the western hemisphere for the spread of Christianity. In 1453, Constantinople was captured by the Turks, bringing to an end the eastern Roman Empire. Greek scholars fled to Italy, bringing along with them their Greek manuscripts. This sparked the Renaissance, which had already begun in the fourteenth century, and paved the way for the Protestant Reformation of the sixteenth century. Up to this time, all education in western Europe was in Latin. But now men began to study Greek. Then came the advent of printing (about 1456), so that this new learning could be widely disseminated. All these together mark the change from medieval to modern times.

For the next few centuries Christian scholars sought to understand the Greek New Testament on the basis of classical Greek. Then the discovery of large amounts of papyri from around the time of Christ added a whole new dimension to the study of New Testament Greek. This is reflected in lexicons and reference works written during the last 50 years. But increasingly it is being recognized today that the most important single source for our understanding of the New Testament is the Septuagint Old Testament. This was the Bible used by the writers of the New Testament and read by the earliest believers.

b. Later Greek Versions. In fact, the Septuagint became known in the first century more and more as the Bible of the Christians. From it they derived their Messianic proof texts and their arguments against Judaism. So in spite of the fact that the Septuagint was very popular among the Greek-speaking Jews of the Diaspora, it was felt that new Greek translations must be made.

There were three of these. The first was that of Aquila, a proselyte of Pontus. In A.D. 128 he produced a slavishly literal translation of the Hebrew text. At about the same time the Septuagint was revised by Theodotion, with careful comparison of the Hebrew text. Toward the end of the second century Symmachus made a third translation, actually a paraphrase in rather elegant style.

Latin Versions

a. Old Latin. This name includes all the Latin versions of both the Old and New Testaments made before Jerome's revision at the end of the fourth century. Apparently the first one was produced in North Africa in the latter part of the second century. (It was at this time that Tertullian of North Africa became the first church father to write in Latin.) The Old Testament was translated from the Septuagint, not the Hebrew, while the New Testament was done from the original Greek.

In the third century several Old Latin versions were circulating in Italy, Gaul (France), and Spain. Many of these were in crude vernacular style, instead of the literary language of that day. This is probably what led Augustine to say that "in the early days of the faith, every man who happened to gain possession of a Greek manuscript and who imagined that he had any facility in both languages (however slight that may be) dared to make a translation."[1]

b. The Vulgate. It was probably in A.D. 382 that Pope Damasus requested Eusebius Heironymus, known today as Jerome, to revise the current Latin versions of the Bible. The next year this scholar gave the pope his first installment, the four Gospels, indicating that he had checked the Old Latin against the Greek. In the Old Testament he made use of the Septuagint, but finally decided he should translate the Hebrew original. To do this he secured the aid of Jewish rabbis.

Because he made many changes in the Old Latin, Jerome was assailed by angry critics. Even Augustine was afraid that by using the Hebrew text of the Old Testament instead of the Greek translation Jerome was calling in doubt the divine inspiration of the Septuagint! But the superior worth of the new revision was finally recognized, so that it came to be called the Vulgate, or "common" version.

Syriac Versions

The Syriac is a Semitic language. Used in western Mesopotamia, it was closely related to the Aramaic dialect used in Palestine at the time of Christ.

a. Old Syriac. Like the Old Latin, the Old Syriac rose in the second century. About the same time, around A.D. 170, Tatian produced his famous *Diatessaron*, a harmony of the Gospels in one continuous narrative. This is one of the proofs that our four Gospels, and no others, were ac-

---

[1] *On Christian Doctrine*, II, 13.

cepted at that time, since only material from the four Gospels is used.

b. The Peshitta. Just as the Old Latin had been corrupted by many hands, so had the Old Syriac. So about the end of the fourth or beginning of the fifth century, a Peshitta ("simple") version was made. It became the popular version for the Syriac churches, as the Vulgate did for the Latin.

During the early centuries many other versions were made, such as the Coptic (Egyptian), Gothic, Armenian, Ethiopic, and later, Arabic. But we pass over all these to come immediately to what concerns us most, the translations into the English language.

English Versions

a. Early Beginnings. In his *Ecclesiastical History* the Venerable Bede tells how Caedmon (died 680) was a cowherd at the monastery of Whitby. One night in a dream he saw a man who told him to sing a song of the creation. In the morning he astonished everyone with his poetic gift. Brought into the monastery, Caedmon was told stories from the Bible and proceeded to turn them into Anglo-Saxon verse. He is said to have sung all the history of Genesis, the story of the Exodus, as well as the great truths of the New Testament. Some think that only his original hymn of creation survives with certainty today. Before the death of Bede in 735 the four Gospels had all appeared in Anglo-Saxon. Bede himself is credited with having translated the Gospel of John. King Alfred (848-901) was much interested in the Bible and saw to it that a new translation of Psalms was made. Several other versions of parts of the Bible appeared in the following centuries.

b. Wyclif's Bible (1382). This was the first complete Bible in English. It was made from the Latin Vulgate, not the Greek. Wyclif's concern was to give the laity of his day a Bible they could read, as a part of the greatly needed effort to reform the Church. In fact, he is called the "morning star of the Reformation," for his English Bible did much to prepare the way for that movement in Britain. To get the Bible to the common people, Wyclif organized the "Poor Priests," or Lollards, who went everywhere teaching the Bible and delivering it to the laymen. Nearly 200 copies of Wyclif's Bible, or revisions of it, are still found in various libraries and museums. And this in spite of the fact that they were very expensive, being copied by hand, and that the authorities had passed a ruling that anyone who read the Scriptures in English "should forfeit land, catel, life, and goods from their heyres forever."[2]

John Wyclif, a graduate of Oxford, became master of Balliol College there and was considered to be the most able theologian on the faculty. Yet in 1411, Archbishop Arundel wrote to the pope: "This pestilent and wretched John Wyclif, of cursed memory, that son of the old serpent . . . endeavoured by every means to attack the very faith and sacred doctrine of Holy Church, devising—to fill up the measure of his malice—the expedient of a new translation of the Scriptures into the mother tongue."[3]

Another contemporary with equal venom wrote his feelings as follows:

> This Master John Wyclif translated from Latin into English—the Angle not the angel speech—the Gospel that Christ gave to the clergy and doctors of the Church . . . so that by his means it has become vulgar and more open to laymen and women who can read than it usually is to quite learned clergy of good intelligence. And so the

[2] J. R. Branton, "Versions, English," *The Interpreter's Dictionary of the Bible* (New York: Abingdon Press, 1962), IV, 761.

[3] Quoted in G. W. Lampe (ed.), *The Cambridge History of the Bible* (Cambridge: University Press, 1969), II, 388.

pearl of the Gospel is scattered abroad and trodden under-
foot by swine.[4]

Wyclif died in 1384, soon after finishing the translation. In 1428 his bones were disinterred and burned, and the
ashes scattered on the river. But someone observed that as
the waters of the river Swift carried these ashes onward
to the Avon and Severn, and the Severn to the sea, so his
influence spread far and wide.

c. *Tyndale's New Testament* (1526). At some time
around 1456 the first book ever printed in Europe on mova-
ble type came off the press. It was the famous Gutenburg
Bible, named after its printer, and was a copy of the Latin
Vulgate. It was not until 70 years later that the first printed
English New Testament appeared, translated by Tyndale.

William Tyndale received his M.A. at Oxford and then
went to Cambridge, where Erasmus had arrived in 1511
to teach Greek. When he left there he soon became known
as a keen debater. One day a learned man said to him: "We
were better be without God's law than the Pope's." Tyndale's
famous reply was: "If God spare my lyfe, ere many yeares
I wyl cause a boye that dryveth the plough shall know more
of the scripture than thou doest."[5] This promise was fulfilled.

At this time he wrote that he "perceaved by expery-
ence how that it was impossible to stablysh the laye people
in any truth excepte the scripture were playnly layde before
their eyes in their mother tonge," and added, "which thynge
onlye moved me to translate the New Testament."[6]

So he went to London, hoping to get support from the
bishop there. Turned down by him, he found a home with
a prosperous merchant, Monmouth. For sheltering the

[4]*Ibid.*
[5]J. R. Branton, *op. cit.,* IV, 761.
[6]*Ibid.*

"heretic," this businessman was later arrested and thrown into the Tower of London.

Frustrated in his purpose, Tyndale wrote: "In London I abode almoste an yere . . . and understode at the laste not only that there was no rowme in my lorde of londons palace to translate the new testament, but also that there was no place to do it in al englonde."[7] So he left England. After a visit with Luther at Wittenberg and the receipt of funds from Monmouth, he hurried to Cologne in 1525 and began printing his translation of the New Testament.

But difficulties still dogged his steps. Cochlaeus, an enemy of the Reformation, invited some printers to his home, plied them with wine until they talked too freely, and learned from them that 3,000 English copies of "The Lutheran New Testament" were right then on the press, being prepared for shipment to England. He obtained an injunction against the project. Tyndale and his assistant took a boat up the Rhine to Worms, carrying with them the sheets already printed. Here the printing was resumed. "The first complete printed New Testament in English appeared towards the end of February 1526, and copies were beginning to reach England about a month later."[8]

The reaction in England was twofold. As the copies of the New Testament were smuggled in, wrapped in merchandise, the people bought them eagerly. But the ecclesiastical authorities became violent in their opposition. The bishop of London said he could find 2,000 errors in Tyndale's New Testament, and he ordered all copies to be burned. By "errors" he actually meant changes from the Latin Vulgate! The archbishop raised funds with which to buy them and burn them publicly. Cochlaeus, the old foe, made this classic speech: "The New Testament translated into

[7] Ibid.

[8] F. F. Bruce, The English Bible: A History of Translations (New York: Oxford University Press, 1961), p. 31.

the vulgar [common] tongue is in truth the food of death, the fuel of sin, the veil of malice, the pretext of false liberty, the protection of disobedience, the corruption of discipline, the depravity of morals, the termination of concord, the death of honesty, the well-spring of vices, the disease of virtues, the instigation of rebellion, the milk of pride, the nourishment of contempt, the death of peace, the destruction of charity, the enemy of unity, the murderer of truth."[9] It was a serious crime to translate the Word of God into the language of the common people!

Because of the strong opposition only three fragments now remain of the 18,000 copies printed between 1526 and 1528. But the value of Tyndale's New Testament can hardly be overestimated. It was made from the original Greek, not the Vulgate. Tyndale was a real scholar. Besides Greek he knew Latin, Hebrew, French, Spanish, Italian, German. His New Testament had a profound influence on subsequent translations. Herbert Gordon May writes:

> It has been estimated that one third of the King James Version of the New Testament is worded as Tyndale had it, and that even in the remaining two thirds the general literary structure set by Tyndale has been retained. Some scholars have said that ninety percent of Tyndale is reproduced in the King James Version of the New Testament.[10]

Having finished his New Testament translation, Tyndale started translating the Old Testament from the original Hebrew. In 1530 he published the Pentateuch. Twice (1534, 1535) he revised his translation of the New Testament, seeking to make it as nearly perfect as possible. Apparently he also translated from Joshua to Chronicles, though this was not published until after his death.

[9]Branton, *op. cit.*, p. 762.
[10]*Our English Bible in the Making* (Philadelphia: The Westminister Press, 1952), p. 26.

In May, 1535, a supposed friend had Tyndale treacherously arrested in Antwerp, Belgium, where he was living in exile from England. He was imprisoned for over a year. While in prison he wrote a letter in Latin to the governor of the castle where he was held. It bears a striking resemblance to Paul's words written from prison in Rome (II Tim. 4:9-21). We quote a part of the English translation:

> Wherefore I beg . . . that if I am to remain here through the winter, you will request the commissary to have the kindness to send me, from the goods of mine which he has, a warmer cap; for I suffer greatly from cold in the head, and am much afflicted by a perpetual catarrh, which is much increased in this cell; a warmer coat also, for this which I have is very thin . . . My overcoat is worn out; my shirts are also worn out . . . And I ask to be allowed to have a lamp in the evening; it is indeed wearisome sitting alone in the dark. But most of all I beg . . . to have the Hebrew Bible, Hebrew grammar, and Hebrew dictionary, that I may pass the time in that study.[11]

There is no indication that this request was granted. In 1536, Tyndale was condemned for heresy, strangled, and burned at the stake. His famous last words were: "Lord, open the King of England's eyes." He did not have the satisfaction of knowing that some months before this King Henry VIII had already given his permission for the circulation in England of the Coverdale Bible, which incorporated most of Tyndale's work.

d. Coverdale's Bible (1535). The first complete printed English Bible was issued by Myles Coverdale in 1535. Educated at Cambridge, he had to live on the Continent while he worked on his translation from 1528 to 1534. He was not the original scholar that Tyndale was. Fortunately, his New Testament is only a revision of Tyndale's, and he

[11]Quoted in F. F. Bruce, *op. cit.*, pp. 51-52.

leaned heavily on the latter's translation of the Pentateuch. But Coverdale must be given much credit for his efforts to make the whole Bible available in English. To this task he devoted much of his adult life.

e. The Matthew Bible (1537). This Bible, which was printed on the Continent under the pen name of Thomas Matthew, was largely a revision of Tyndale's material. It was actually the work of John Rogers, to whom Tyndale turned over his translations when he was imprisoned. Rogers himself was later burned at the stake.

f. The Great Bible (1539). Thomas Cromwell asked Coverdale to prepare another version, based on the Matthew Bible. The measure of Coverdale's devotion to the Word of God is shown by the fact that he was willing to see his own Bible set aside in order to gain wider circulation for a new version.

The printing was begun in Paris, where better presses and paper were available. In spite of the fact that the French king had licensed the project, the Inquisition stopped the printing and attempted to seize the pages already completed. But the type, presses, and workmen were finally moved to London, where the work was finished.

It was called the Great Bible because of its size. The pages measured 16½ by 11 inches. This Bible became the first authorized English version; the 1540 edition had on the title page: "This is the Byble apoynted to the use of the churches." The next year the king issued a proclamation "for the Byble of the largest and greatest volume to be had in every church."

Copies of the Great Bible were placed in the churches, chained to a lectern so that they would not be stolen. People gathered eagerly around these to hear the Word of God read aloud. This activity even went on during the sermon, much to the annoyance of the parsons! The enthusiastic response of the people is shown in the fact that seven print-ings of this Bible were made within three years.

In the same year (1539) the *Taverner Bible* appeared. Taverner was a layman, a graduate of Oxford with an excellent knowledge of Greek. So while he reprinted the Old Testament of the Matthew Bible with little change, he made many revisions in the New Testament.

g. *The Geneva Bible* (1560). The period between 1539 and 1560 was a hectic one for the new English Bibles and their promoters. Under heavy Roman Catholic pressure King Henry VIII reversed his tolerant attitude. In 1543 an act of Parliament forbade using all translations bearing the name of Tyndale. No working man or woman was to read the Bible, on pain of imprisonment.

The next king, Edward VI, was a strong Protestant and sought to restore the Bible to the common people. Archbishop Cranmer supported him in this. Unfortunately, Edward's reign was short (1547-53). He was succeeded by Queen Mary, a fanatical Roman Catholic. During her violent reign of five years no less than 300 Protestant reformers were put to death, including Cranmer and Rogers.

Coverdale escaped to the Continent and joined the band of vigorous Protestants at Geneva. There a group of scholars worked "night and day for two and a half years" to produce the Geneva Bible. It was the first complete English Bible to be divided into verses. It also contained many helpful notes for the common reader. With good reason it became the people's book in England and Scotland. In fact, it was the first Bible to be published in the latter country. The Scottish Parliament passed an act that every home that could afford it should possess a copy of the Bible.

The Geneva version was the Bible of John Bunyan and William Shakespeare. It was also the Bible of the Pilgrim Fathers. It is sometimes called the "Breeches Bible" because it translated Genesis 3:7—"They sewed fig leaves together and made themselves breeches."

As in Coverdale's Bible, the Apocrypha was placed between the Old and New Testament as an appendix. But the Geneva reformers were careful to state that these books were not "to be read and expounded publicly in the Church, neither yet served to prove any point of Christian religion . . ."

h. The Bishops' Bible (1568). For some years there were two main Bibles in England. The Geneva was the Bible of the people and the Great Bible was for the pulpits in the churches. Finally Archbishop Parker ordered a revision of the Great Bible, hoping it would take the place of both versions. Because many of the scholars who did the work of revising were bishops, it was called the Bishops' Bible.

Unfortunately, the bishops loved their Latin. So for "love" in First Corinthians 13 in the earlier versions, they substituted "charity," from the Latin Vulgate *caritas*. This sad mistake was carried over into the King James Version, which was a revision of the bishops' Bible.

i. The Douay-Rheims Version (1609-10). The Roman Catholic leaders were much disturbed by the fact that Protestants were becoming very familiar with the Bible in their own mother tongue. So—unwillingly, as they themselves stated—they decided to put out an English version of their own. The New Testament was completed in 1582 at Rheims, France. The Old Testament was published, 1609-10, at Douay, in Flanders. As would be expected, they were both translated from the Latin Vulgate, the official Catholic Bible.

The translation was wooden and often obscure. Latinisms abound. For instance, it speaks of "supersubstantial" bread and says of one person that he "exinanited himself."

One particularly objectionable feature is the use of "do penance" for "repent."

j. The King James Version (1611). When James VI of Scotland became James I of England (following the death of Queen Elizabeth I in 1603), he called the churchmen together for a conference at Hampton Court (1604). There Dr. John Reynolds, a prominent Puritan leader and president of Corpus Christi College, Oxford, proposed this resolution: "That a translation be made of the whole Bible, as consonant as can be to the original Hebrew and Greek; and this to be set out and printed, without any marginal notes, and only to be used in all Churches of England in time of divine service."

The bishop of London (later Archbishop of Canterbury) objected that "if every man's humour were followed, there would be no end of translating." But King James heartily approved of the resolution and actively promoted the work. By July of 1604 he says that he had "appointed certain learned men to the number of four and fifty for the translating of the Bible." But only 47 names are on the list of those who actually worked on the translation. They were divided into six panels, with three panels for the Old Testament, two for the New Testament, and one for the Apocrypha. Two groups met at Oxford, two at Cambridge, and two at Westminster.

Fifteen ground rules were set up to be followed by the translators. The first one read: "The Bishop's Bible to be followed, and as little altered as the truth of the original will permit." It is clear that this was to be a revision of the Bishops' Bible. Interestingly, it was specified that use should be made of the Tyndale, Matthew, Coverdale, or Great Bible when any of these agreed more closely with the original text than did the Bishops' Bible.

The rules further called for close cooperation between the members of each group. When the work was finished, two members from each of the three centers met as a committee to go over the final translation before it was printed. Thus the effort was made to assure a job well done. The actual work of translation took four years (1607-11).

It is often assumed that the King James Version, as it is called, has come down to us exactly in its original form. This is not true. The fact is that the original edition of the King James Version would make difficult reading for the average American today. (See photographic facsimile.) In 1613, only two years after it was first published, over 300 variations were introduced. Another revision came out in 1629 and still another in 1638. But it was the revision made at Oxford in 1769 that modernized its spelling so that it can be read with some ease in our day. This is essentially the version we now have.

There was one rule given the original translators that they failed to follow, and their mistake was never corrected. They were told to use the commonly known form of proper names. But the King James Version has "Isaiah" in the Old Testament and "Esaias" in the New, "Jeremiah" and "Jeremias," "Elijah" and "Elias," "Elisha" and "Eliseus," "Hosea" and "Osee," "Jonah" and "Jonas." Whenever one is reading the King James New Testament in public he should always change these odd forms to the familiar names of the Old Testament, so that the listeners will know about whom he is speaking.

The main strength of the King James Version was its beautiful Elizabethan English prose. For this reason it became the most widely used English Bible for three centuries. William Lyons Phelps, famous teacher of literature at Yale University, once said that Shakespeare and the King James Version standardized the English language.

Often the King James Version is referred to as "The Authorized Version" (AV). But this is incorrect. The Great Bible of 1539 and the Bishop's Bible of 1560 were both authorized versions. The King James Version of 1611 carries on the title page: "Appointed to be read in the churches." But there is no record that any official action was ever taken to authorize this.

In view of the opposition to some recent versions of the Bible, it is interesting to note that the King James Version also suffered similarly at first. Dr. Hugh Broughton, one of the greatest Greek and Hebrew scholars of that day, wrote his feelings about it:

> The late Bible . . . was sent me to censure: which bred in me a sadness that will grieve me while I breathe, it is so ill done. Tell His Majesty that I had rather be rent in pieces with wild horses, than any such translation by my consent should be urged upon poor churches . . . The new edition crosseth me. I require it to be burnt.[12]

Some critics of the King James Version went even further in their denunciations. They accused the translators of blasphemy and called them "damnable corruptors" of God's Word.[13]

The Pilgrims who came to this country in 1620 refused to have anything to do with the King James Version. They much preferred the Geneva Bible and continued to use it. In fact, it was not until 1777 that the New Testament of the King James Version was published in America. The complete Bible finally came out in 1782.

Gradually the King James Version supplanted the Geneva Bible in the new nation of the United States. After some years it became the dominant Bible there, as in England.

Perhaps some reader has wondered why most people, when repeating the Lord's Prayer, say, "And forgive us our trespasses, as we forgive those who trespass against us."

---

[12]*Ibid.*, p. 107.
[13]Geddes Mac Gregor, *The Bible in the Making* (Philadelphia: J. B. Lippincott Co., 1959), p. 187.

This often becomes awkward in public worship when some people use the shorter form found in our King James Version, "And forgive us our debts, as we forgive our debtors." Where did the other come from?

The answer is that in the *Book of Common Prayer* of the Church of England the Scripture quotations were taken from the Coverdale Bible and were never revised to conform to the King James Version.

It is unfortunate that our present copies of the King James Version carry in the front of them the dedication to King James, which is full of false flattery and is entirely worthless today, and omit the original Preface, "The Translators to the Readers." In this the wise scholars expressed their dismay at the prevailing attitude of people toward a new translation of the Bible. They wrote:

> Zeal to promote the common good, whether it be by devising anything ourselves, or revising that which hath been laboured by others, deserveth certainly much respect and esteem, but yet findeth but cold entertainment in the world. It is welcomed with suspicion instead of love, and with emulation instead of thanks: and if there be any hole left for cavil to enter, (and cavil, if it do not find a hole, will make one) is sure to be misconstrued, and in danger to be condemned. This will easily be granted by as many as know history, or have any experience. For, was there ever anything projected, that savoured any way of newness of renewing, but the same endured many a storm of gainsaying, or opposition?

It is obvious that people of the seventeenth century took the same attitude as people of the twentieth century toward new translations of the Bible!

In many ways the King James translators did a magnificent job. They put the Bible into a sort of poetical prose that has sung its way across three and a half centuries. There is a rhythmic beauty in the language of the King James Version which will always afford pleasure to many readers.

But this should not blind us to an important fact underscored by C. S. Lewis in his little book *The Literary Impact of the Authorized Version.* He says that "those who read the Bible as literature do not read the Bible."[14] He declares that the Bible is "not merely a sacred book but a book so remorselessly and continuously sacred that it does not invite, it excludes or repels the merely aesthetic approach."[15] To appreciate these statements one must remember that C. S. Lewis was not a preacher or theologian but a famous teacher of English literature at both Oxford and Cambridge universities.

The Bible was not written to entertain but to redeem. That being true, we should seek to have the Scriptures in a translation that conveys to us as exactly and accurately as possible what the original language says.

Questions

1. What is the Septuagint, and what place did it have in the Early Church?

2. What is the Vulgate, and what place has it filled in history?

3. What was the first English Bible, and from what was it translated?

4. Who made the first printed English New Testament, and how did his work influence the King James Version?

5. What was the Bible of the Puritans and Pilgrims?

6. When was the King James Version made, and what was the secret of its final popularity?

---

[14](Philadelphia: Fortress Press, 1963), p. 30.
[15]*Ibid.*, p. 33.

kyngdõ come.Thy will be fulfillet/even inerth
as it is in heven. Oure dayly breed geve vs this
daye.And forgeve vs oure synnes: For even we
forgeve every man that traspaseth vs/and led=
de vs not into temptaciõ/Butt deliver vs from
evyll Amen.

And he sayde vnto thê:which of you shall ha=
ve a frende and shall goo to hym att mydnyght/
and saye vnto hym:frende lende me foure loves
for a frende of myne is come out off the waye to
me/and J haven othynge to sett before hi/And
he with in shall andswer and saye: Trouble me
nott/nowe is the doze shett/and my servauntts
are with me in the chamber/J cannot ryse and
geve thê to the. J saye vnto you:though he woll
not aryse and geve hym/be cause he is his fren=
de: Yet because of hys importunite he woll ryse
and geve him as many as he nedeth.

And J saye vnto you: axe/and yt shalbe ge=
ven you. Seke/and ye shall fynde. knocke/and
it shalbe opened vnto you. For every one that
axeth/receaveth: and he that seketh/fyndeth:
ãd to him that knocketh shall it be openned. Yf
the sonne axe breed off eny off you whichys hys
father:wyll he proffer hym a stone? Or yf he
axe fisshe/wyll he geve hym a serpent?Or yf he
axe an egge:wyll he proffer him a scorpion? Yf
ye thê which are evyll/knowe howe to geve good
gyftes vnto youre chyldren? Howe moche more
shall youre father celestiall/geve a goode sprete
to them/that desire it of hym.

And he was a castynge out a devyll/whyche
was dom. And it folowed when the devyll was

Tyndale's New Testament, 1526

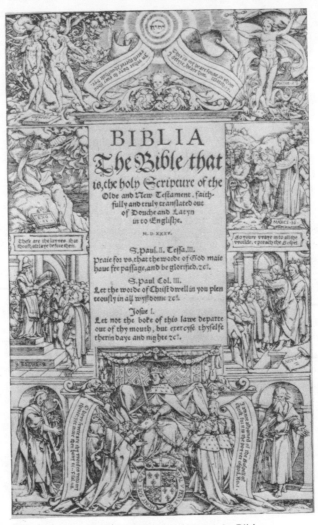

The Title Page of the Coverdale Bible

which ſtryped him out of his clothes, and wounded him, and wente their waye, and leſs him half deed. And by chaûce there came downe a preſt the ſame waye: and whan he ſawe him, he paſſed by. And likewyſe a Leuite, whã he came nye vnto the ſame place and ſawe him, he paſſed by. But a Samaritane was goynge his iourney, and came that waye, and whan he ſawe him, he had compaſſion vpon him, wente vnto him, boumde vp his woundes, and poured oyle and wyne therin, and lifte him vp vpon his beaſt, and brought him into the ynne, and made prouyſion for him. Vpon the next daye whan he departed, he toke out two pens, and gaue them to the ooſt, and ſayde vnto him: Take cure of him, and what ſo euer thou ſpendeſt more, I wil paye it the, whan I come agayne. Which of theſe thre now thinkeſt thou, was neghboure vnto him, that fell amonge the murtherers? He ſayde: He that ſhewed mercy vpon him. Then ſayde Jeſus vnto him: Go thy waye then, and do thou likewyſe.

It fortuned as they were, that he entred into a towne, where there was a woman named Martha, which receaued him into hir houſe. And ſhe had a ſiſter, called Mary, which ſat hir downe at Jeſus fete, and herkened vnto his worde. But Martha made hir ſelf moch to do, for to ſerue him. And ſhe ſtepte vnto him, and ſayde: LORDE, careſt thou not, that my ſiſter letteth me ſerue alone? Byd her therfore, that ſhe helpe me. But Jeſus anſwered, and ſayde vnto her: Martha Martha, thou takeſt thought, and combreſt thy ſelf aboute many thinges: there is but one thinge nedefull. Mary hath choſen a good parte, which ſhal not be taken awaye from her.

The XI. Chapter.

And it fortuned that he was in a place, and prayed. And whan he had ceaſſed, one of his diſciples ſayde vnto him: LORDE, teach vs to praye, as Jhon alſo taught his diſciples. He ſayde vnto the: Whan ye praye, ſaye: O oure father which art in heauen, halowed be thy name. Thy kyngdome come. Thy wil be fulfilled vpon earth, as it is in heauen. Geue vs this daye oure daylie bred. And forgeue vs oure ſynnes, for we alſo forgeue all them that are detters vnto vs. And lede vs not in to temptacion, but delyuer vs from euell.

And he ſayde vnto them: Which of you is it that hath a frende, and ſhulde go to him at mydnighte, and ſaye vnto him: frende, lende me thre loaues, for a frende of myne is come to me out of the waye, and I haue nothinge to ſet before him: and he within ſhulde anſwere and ſaye: Diſquyete me not, the dore is ſhut allready, and my children are with me in the chamber, I can not ryſe, and geue the. I ſaye vnto you: and though he wolde not aryſe and geue him, becauſe he is his frende, yet becauſe of his vnſhamefaſt begginge he wolde aryſe, and geue him as many as he nedeth.

And I ſaye vnto you alſo: Axe, and it ſhal be geuen you: Seke, and ye ſhal fynde: knocke, and it ſhalbe opened vnto you. For whoſo euer axeth, receaueth: and he that ſeketh, fyndeth: and to him that knocketh, ſhal it be opened. Yf the ſonne axe bred of eny of you that is a father, wyl he geue him a ſtone therfore? Or yf he axe a fyſhe, wyl he for the fiſh offre him a ſerpent? Or yf he axe an egg, wyl he profer him a ſcorpion? Yf ye then which are euell, can geue youre children good giftes, how moch more ſhal the father of heauen geue the holy ſprete vnto them that are him?

And he droue out a deuell that was dom me: and it came to paſſe whan the deuell was departed out, the domme ſpake, and the people wondred. But ſome of them ſaye: He dryueth out the deuels, thorow Beelzebub the cheſe of the deuels. The other tempted him, and deſyred a token of him from heauen. But he knewe their thoughtes, and ſayde vnto them: Euery kyngdome deuyded within it ſelf ſhal be deſolate, and one houſe ſhal fall vpõ another. Yf Sathan then be at variaunce within himſelf, how ſhal his kyngdome endure? Becauſe ye ſaye, that I dryue out deuels thorow Beelzebub.

And yf I dryue out deuels thorow Beelzebul, by whom the do youre children dryue them out? Therfore ſhall they be youre iudges. But yf I caſt out the deuels by the fynger of God, then is the kyngdome of God come vnto you.

Whan a ſtronge harneſſed man kepeth his houſe, that he poſſeſſeth is in peace: but whan a ſtronger then he commeth vpõ him, and ouercommeth him he taketh frõ him all his wapens, wherin he truſted, and deuydeth the ſpoyle. He that is not with me, is agaynſt me: and he that ga-

SS ij

The Coverdale Bible, 1535

prophetes & kynges haue desyred to se those thynges whych ye se, and haue not sene thē: and to heare those thynges whych ye heare, and haue not hearde them.

And beholde a certayne lawer stode vp, ād tempted hym, saying: ✶ Master, what shall I do, to inheret eternall lyfe: he sayde vnto hym: What is wrytten i the lawe? How redest thou? And he answered ād sayde: ✶ loue the Lorde thy God, with all thy hert, & with all thy soule, & wyth all thy strength, & with all thy mynde: and thy neyghbour as thy selfe. And he sayde vnto hym. Thou hast āswered ryght. Thys do, ād thou shalt lyue. But he wyllynge to iustyfye hym selfe, sayde vnto Iesus. And who is my neyghbour?

Iesus answered, & sayde, A certayne man descended from Hierusalem to Hierico, & fell amōg theues, whych robbed him of hys rayment & wounded hym, & departed, leauynge hym halfe deed. And it chaunced, ȳ ther came downe a certayne Preste ȳ same waye: and whē he sawe hi, he passed by. And lyke wyse a Leuite, whē he wēt nye to ȳ place, came ād loked on hi, & passed by. But a certayne Samaritane, as he iorneyed, came vnto hym: & when he sawe hym, he had cōpassyō on hym: & wēt to, & bounde vp his woundes, & poured i oyle & wyne, & set hym on hys awne beaste, & brought hym to a cōmē ynne, & made prouisyon for him. And on ȳ morow, whē he departed, he toke out two pēce, & gaue thē to ȳ host, & sayd vnto hi: Take cure of hi, & whatsoeuer ȳ spedest moare, whē I come agayne I will recōpēce the. Whych now of these thre thynkest ȳ, was neyghbour vnto hym ȳ fell among the theues? And he sayde: he that shewed mercy on hym. Then sayde Iesus vnto hym: Go, and do thou lyke wyse.

It fortuned that as they went, he entred into a certayne towne. And a certayne womā named Martha, receaued him ito her house. And thys woman had a syster called Mary, whych also sate at Iesus fete, & heard hys worde. But Martha was cōbred about moche seruynge, & stode & sayd: lorde, doest ȳ not care, that my syster hath left me to serue alone? Byd her therfore, ȳ she helpe me. And Iesus answered, & sayde vnto her: Martha, Martha, ȳ art carefull, and troubled about many thiges: verely—— one is nedfull. Mary hath chosen the good parte, whych shall not be taken awaye from her.

The .xi. Chapter.

Christ teacheth his disciples to praye, he wasteth out a deuyll, & reboketh the blasphemous Pharises. They requyre signes & tokens. He eateth with the Pharise, & reproueth the prouerbe of the Pharises, Scribes and hypocrites.

And it fortuned as he was prayinge in a certayne place: whē he ceased, one of his disciples sayde vnto hym: Lorde, teache vs to praye, as Iohn also taught hys disciples. And he sayde vnto them: when ye praye, saye. ✶ Oure father which art i heauen, halowed be thy name. Thy kyngdome come. Thy will be fulfylled, euē in erth also as it is in heauē. Oure dayly bred geue vs thys daye. And forgeue vs our synnes: for euē we forgeue euery man that trespaseth vs. And Leade vs not ito temptacyon. But delyuer vs from euyll.

And he sayde vnto them: yf any of you shal haue a frende, ād shal go to hym at myd nyght, and saye vnto hym, frende: lende me thre loaues, for a frende of myne is come out of the waye to me, and I haue nothynge to set before hym, and he wythin answere, and saye: trouble me not, the dore is now shut, and my chyldren are wyth me in the chamber, I cannot ryse and geue the. I saye vnto you, though he wyll not aryse ād geue hym, because he is hys frēde: yet because of hys importunite he will ryse, ād geue hym as many as he nedeth. And I saye vnto you: ✶ aske, and it shalbe geuen you. Seke, and ye shall fynde. knocke, & it shalbe opened vnto you. for—— euery one ȳ asketh, receaueth: and he that seketh, fyndeth: & to hym ȳ knocketh, shall it be opened. Yf a sōne shall a syke bred of eny of you that is a father, wyll he geue him a stone? Or yf he aske fisshe, wyll he for fysshe geue hym a serpent? Or yf he aske an egge, wyll he offer hi a scorpion? Yf ye then beyng euill, can geue good giftes vnto your chyldren, how moch moare shall your father of heauen geue the holy sprete to them, that desyre it of hym?

And he was castynge out a deuyll, and the same was dōmme. And whē he had cast out the deuill, the dōme spake, & the people wondred. But some of them sayd: ✶ he casteth out deuyls thorow Beelzebub the chefe of the deuyls. And other tempted hym and requyred of hym a sygne from heauen. But he knowing their thoughtes, sayde vnto them: Euery kyngdom deuyded agaynst it selfe, is desolate: and one house doth fall vpon another. Yf Satan also, be deuyded agaynst hym selfe, how shall hys kyngdome endure? Because ye saye, that I cast out deuyls thorow Beelzebub. If I, by the helpe of Beelzebub cast out deuyls, by whose helpe do youre chyldrē cast them out. Therfore shall they be your iudges. But yf I, wt the fynger of God cast out deuyls, no doubte the kyngdome of God is come vpon you.

When a strōge mā armed watcheth hys house, the thynges that he possesseth are in peace. But when a stronger then he cōmeth vpon hym, and ouercōmeth hym, he taketh from him all hys harnes, wherin he trusted, and deuydeth hys goodes. He that is not wt me, is agaynst me. And he ȳ gathereth not wt me, scattereth abrode.

Dd v   ✶When the

*Mat.11,21.

13 ¶ Wo *be to thee, Chorazin: wo be to thee, Beth faida: for if the miracles had bene done in Tyrus & Sidon, which haue bene done in you, they had a great while ago ne repented, fitting * in facke clothe and affhes.

*k Which were the fignes of repentance.

14 Therefore it fhalbe eafier for Tyrus, & Sidon, at the iudgement, then for you.

15 And thou, Capernaum, which art exalted to heauē, fhalt be thruſt downe to hel.

16 ¶ He that heareth you, heareth me: & he that defpifeth you, defpifeth me: and he that defpifeth me, defpifeth him that fent me.

17 ¶ And the feuentie turned againe with ioye, faying, Lord, euen the deuils are fubdued to vs throughthy Name.

18 And he faid vnto them, I fawe ᵐ Satan, like lightening, fall downe from heauen.

19 Beholde, I giue vnto you power to treade on ferpents, and fcorpions, and ouer all the power of the enemie, & nothing fhal hurt you.

20 Neuertheles, in this reioyce not, that ỹ fpirits are fubdued vnto you: but rather reioyce, becaufe your names are written in heauen.

21 ¶ That fame houre reioyced Iefus in the ſpirit, and faid, I confeffe vnto thee, Father, Lord of heauen & earth, that thou haſt hid thefe things from the * wife and learned, and haſt reueiled them to babes: euen fo, Father, becaufe it fo pleafed thee.

22 Then he turned to his difciples, and faid, All things are ᵖ giuen me of my Father: and ᵣ no man knoweth who the Sonne is, but the Father: nether who the Father is, faue the ᵀ Sonne, and he to whome the Sonne wil reueile him.

23 ¶ And he returned to his difciples, and faid fecretly, * Bleffed are the eyes, which fe that ye fe.

24 For I tell you that manie Prophetes & Kings haue defired to fe thofe things, which ye fe, and haue not fene them: and to heare thofe things, which ye heare, & haue not heard them.

25 ¶ * Then beholde, a certeine expounder of the Law ſtode vp, and tempted him, faying, Maſter, what fhal I do, to inherite eternal life?

26 And he faid vnto him, What is written in the Law? how readeſt thou?

27 And he anfwered, and faid, * Thou fhalt loue thy Lord God with all thine heart, & with all thy foule, & with all thy ſtrength, & with all thy thoght, * & thy neighbour as thy felf.

28 Then he faid vnto him, Thou haſt anfwered right: this do, & thou fhalt liue.

29 But he willing to ᵗ iuſtifie him felf, faid vnto Iefus, Who ᵘ is then my neighbour?

30 And Iefus anfwered, and faid, A certeine man went downe from Ieruſalem to Iericho, and fell among theues, and they robbed him of his rayment, and wounded him, & departed, leauing him halfe dead.

31 And by ᵃ chance there came downe a certeine ᵇ Prieſt that fame way, and when he fawe him, he paffed by on the other fide.

32 And likewife alfo a Leuite, when he was come nere to the place, went and loked on him, and paffed by on the other fide.

33 Then a certeine ᶜ Samaritan as he iourneyed, came nere vnto him, and when he fawe him, he had compaffion on him,

34 And went to him, & bounde vp his woūdes, and powred in oyle and wine, and put him on his owne beaſt, and broght him to an ynne, and made prouifion for him.

35 And on the morowe when he departed, he toke out ᵉ two pence, and gaue them to the hoſte, and faid vnto him, Take care of him, and whatſ euer thou fpendeſt more, when I come againe, I wil recompenfe thee.

36 Which now of thefe three, thinkeſt thou, was neighbour vnto him that fell among the theues?

37 And he faid, He that fhewed mercie on him. Then faid Iefus vnto him, Go, ᶠ and do thou likewife.

38 ¶ Now it came to paffe as they wēt, that he entred into a certeine towne, and a certeine woman named Martha, receiued him into her houfe.

39 And fhe had a fifter called Marie, which alfo fate at Iefus fete, and heard his preaching.

40 But Martha was combred about muche feruing, and came to him, & faid, Maſter, doeſt thou not care that my fiſter hathe left me to ferue alone? bid her therefore, that fhe helpe me.

41 And Iefus anfwered, and faid vnto her, Martha, Martha, thou careſt, & art ᵗ troubled about manie things.

42 But one thing is nedeful, Marie hathe chofen the good parte, ᵘ which fhal not be taken away from her.

CHAP. XI.

1 He teacheth his difciples to pray. 14 He driueth out a dumme deuil. 27 And rebuketh the blafphemous Tharifes. 28 He preferreth the fpirituall cognage. 29 They require fignes and tokens. 37 He eateth with the Tharifes, Scribes and hypocrites.

AND fo it was, that as he was praying in a certeine place, when he ceafed, one of his difciples faid vnto him, Maſter, teache vs to praye, as Iohn alfo taught his difciples.

2 * And he faid vnto them, When ye pray, fay, O ᵃ Father, which art in heauē, halowed be thy Name: Thy kingdome come: Let thy wil be done euē in earth, as it is in heauen:

3 Our

28 And he said vnto him, Thou hast answered right: this do, and thou shalt liue.

29 But he willing to iustifie himselfe, said vnto Iesus, And who is my neighbour?

30 And Iesus answering, said, A certaine man went downe from Hierusalem to Iericho, and fell among theeues, which stripped him of his raiment, and wounded him, and departed, leauing him halfe dead.

31 And by chaunce there came downe a certaine Priest that way, and when he saw him, he passed by on the other side.

32 And likewise a Leuite, when hee was at the place, came and looked on him, and passed by on the other side.

33 But a certaine Samaritane as he iourneyed, came where he was: and when hee saw him, hee had compassion on him.

34 And went to him, and bound vp his wounds, powring in oile and wine, and set him on his owne beast, and brought him to an Inne, and tooke care of him.

|| See Mat. 10.3.

35 And on the morrow when he departed, hee tooke out two || pence, and gaue them to the hoste, and saide vnto him, Take care of him, and whatsoeuer thou spendest more, when I come againe, I will repay thee.

36 Which now of these three, thinkest thou, was neighbour vnto him that fell among the theeues?

37 And he said, he that shewed mercie on him. Then said Iesus vnto him, Goe, and doe thou likewise.

38 ¶ Now it came to passe, as they went, that he entred into a certaine village: and a certaine woman named Martha, receiued him into her house.

39 And shee had a sister called Mary, which also sate at Iesus feet, and heard his word:

40 But Martha was cumbred about much seruing, and came to him, and said, Lord, doest thou not care that my sister hath left mee to serue alone? Bid her therefore that she helpe me.

41 And Iesus answered, and saide vnto her, Martha, Martha, thou art carefull, and troubled about many things:

42 But one thing is needefull, and Mary hath chosen that good part, which shall not bee taken away from her.

CHAP. XI.

1 Christ teacheth to pray, and that instantly: 11 assuring that God so will giue vs good things. 14 He casting out a dumbe deuil, rebuketh the blasphemous Pharisees: 28 and sheweth who are blessed: 29 preacheth to the people, 37 and reprehendeth the outward shew of holinesse in the Pharisees, Scribes and Lawyers.

AND it came to passe, that as he was praying in a certaine place, when hee ceased, one of his disciples said vnto him, Lord, teach vs to pray, as Iohn also taught his disciples.

2 And hee said vnto them, When ye pray, say, * Our Father which art in heauen, halowed be thy Name, Thy kingdome come, Thy will be done as in heauen, so in earth.

* Mat. 6. 9.

3 Giue vs || day by day our dayly bread.

|| Or, for the day.

4 And forgiue vs our sinnes: for we also forgiue euery one that is indebted to vs. And lead vs not into temptation, but deliuer vs from euill.

5 And he said vnto them, which of you shall haue a friend, and shall goe vnto him at midnight, and say vnto him, Friend, lend me three loaues.

6 For a friend of mine in his iourney is come to me, and I haue nothing to set before him.

|| Or, out of his way.

7 And he from within shall answere and say, Trouble mee not, the doore is now shut, and my children are with me in bed: I cannot rise and giue thee.

8 I say vnto you, Though he will not rise, and giue him, because he is his friend: yet because of his importunitie, hee will rise and giue him as many as he needeth.

9 * And I say vnto you, Aske, and it shalbe giuen you: seeke, and ye shal find: knocke, and it shalbe opened vnto you.

* Math. 7. 7.

10 For euery one that asketh, receiueth: and he that seeketh, findeth: and to him that knocketh, it shalbe opened.

11 If a sonne shall aske bread of any of you that is a father, will hee giue him a stone? Or if he aske a fish, will he for a fish giue him a serpent?

* Math. 7. 7.

12 Or if he shall ask te an egge, will he offer him a scorpion?

13 If ye then, being euill, know how to giue good gifts vnto your children: how much more shall your heauenly Father

The King James Version, 1611

V

Its Propagation

Oh, for a thousand tongues to sing
   My great Redeemer's praise,
The glories of my God and King,
   The triumphs of His grace!

My gracious Master and my God,
   Assist me to proclaim,
To spread through all the earth abroad,
   The honors of Thy name.

So wrote Charles Wesley over two centuries ago. Little did he dream that within that period of time the Bible would be translated into over a thousand tongues and spread throughout the entire world.

Charles Wesley died in 1788, and his more famous brother John in 1791. The next year, 1792, marks the beginning of the great modern era of world missions. More was done in the evangelization of the whole globe in the next 150 years than had been done in the previous 1,500 years.

William Carey was a Baptist preacher in England. So poor was his congregation that he had to support his family be making shoes. But his heart was burdened for the millions of people in Asia and Africa who had never heard the gospel. Above his cobbler's bench he hung a map of the world, until he could say with John Wesley, "The world is my parish." In spite of the pressure of pastoral duties and working for a living, young Carey mastered Latin, Greek, and Hebrew. One day he preached a sermon on "Expect great things from God; attempt great things for God." Largely as a result, the first Baptist missionary society was founded in 1792. The next year William Carey and his family sailed for India, accompanied by John Thomas, who had lived in Bengal.

Soon after they arrived in India all their property was lost in the Hooghly River. Only his rugged faith in God kept William Carey going. He had to take a job in an indigo factory because funds from the home society failed to come. But this new employment gave him close contact with the nationals, which was invaluable in learning their language. For five years he studied the Bengali and Sanskrit languages.

Finally, at Serampore, he translated the New Testament into Bengali and published it in 1801. For 30 years Carey taught Bengali, Marathi, and Sanscrit. This brought him into contact with leading Indian intellectuals. With their help he was able to translate the Scriptures into all the principal languages of northern Hindustan. He used his salary to establish a press on which these were printed.

The total production of William Carey and his helpers is staggering. He is credited with the translation of the whole Bible into nine languages, the New Testament into 27 more, and smaller portions of Scripture in several others. "The whole number of languages is stated at forty, and we are probably below the truth when we state that the Serampore press, under the auspices chiefly of Dr. Carey, was honored to be the instrument, in about thirty years, of rendering the Word of God accessible to three hundred millions of human beings, or nearly one third of the population of the world."[1]

All mankind is deeply indebted to such men of vision and courage as William Carey. One is tempted to wonder what the history of the nineteenth and twentieth centuries would have been if God had had a hundred Careys to carry on the work of His kingdom.

A few statistics will help to put in bold relief what we have said thus far. Eric N. North, in his introductory essay, "And Now—in a Thousand Tongues," says that "it is estimated that on the eve of the invention of printing only 33 languages—22 European, 7 Asian, 4 African—had had any part of the Bible translated."[2] More surprising is the statement: "But even by 1800 only 71 languages and dialects had seen some printed portion of the Bible—50 in Europe, 13 in Asia, 4 in Africa, 3 in the Americas (Massachusetts, Mohawk, and Arawak), and 1 in Oceania."[3]

Then the picture changed radically. At last the Spirit found a few through whom He could work. North says:

> The next thirty years saw an amazing expansion. Eighty-six languages received some part of the Bible— more than in all the 1800 years before! And sixty-six of these were languages outside of Europe! The missionary movement, with its roots watered and fertilized by the Evangelical Revival of the 18th century, bore this sudden burst of bloom.[4]

One result was that the British and Foreign Bible Society was founded in 1804 and the American Bible Society in 1816. In 1970 the New York Bible Society (founded 1809) added the word "International" to its name, joining the

[1] Quoted in John McClintock and James Strong, *Cyclopaedia of Biblical, Theological and Ecclesiastical Literature* (Grand Rapids, Mich.: Baker Book House, 1968, reprint), II, 121.

[2] (Ed.) *The Book of a Thousand Tongues* (New York: Harper and Brothers, 1938), p. 2.

[3] *Ibid.*

[4] *Ibid.*

forces that are seeking to spread the Bible around the world in as many languages as possible.

By 1938 the translations of Scripture had passed the thousand mark. Of these there were 173 in Europe, 212 in Asia, 345 in Africa, 89 in the Americas, and 189 in Oceania. Now the total figure has gone well over 1,200 languages into which the Bible, in whole or in part, has been translated. The Wycliffe Bible Translators have been most active in this.

We shall take a glimpse at the spread of Bible translations in different world areas. Only a few high points can be noted.

Europe

It has sometimes been said that Martin Luther's most important and lasting contribution to the Protestant Reformation was not his preaching or teaching, but his translation of the Bible into the German of his day. There was a medieval German version available, but it had been made from the Latin Vulgate and was poorly done. Luther had used the Greek text in his lectures on Romans in 1515-16, and the Hebrew in his commentary on Hebrews in 1517-18. So he was prepared for his work of translating the Bible from the original.

The story of his project is a fascinating one. As Luther was returning from the Diet of Worms (1521), where he made his famous "Here I stand" speech, friends were fearful for his life. So they spirited him away to the castle of Wartburg, where he spent the winter in safe hiding.

In December he made a hurried secret trip to Wittenberg. There his friend, Philip Melancthon, advised him to make a translation of the New Testament. When he returned to Wittenberg on March 6, 1522, he already had the first draft completed—in two and a half months! With Melancthon's help he revised it, and it was published in

September of 1522. Luther spent 12 more years, with interruptions due to other duties and illness, translating the Old Testament. Finally his entire German Bible was published in 1534 and became a major bulwark of the Reformation.

Of the literary significance of this translation Hans Volz says:

> Luther's Bible was a literary event of the first magnitude, for it is the first work of art in German prose. . . . the Bible first became a real part of the literary heritage of the German people with Luther. . . . in the history of the language his version is also a factor whose significance cannot be overestimated in the development of the vocabulary of modern literary German.[5]

The average American has no idea how many languages are spoken in Europe, even today. It has already been noted that by 1938 some of the Scripture had been translated into no less than 173 languages of that continent.

But, at least, everybody in the British Isles uses English. Well, not quite. Many people in Wales cling to their native Welsh, as we all saw when Prince Charles was inaugurated as the Prince of Wales. The earliest Welsh Bible appeared over 350 years ago. The New Testament was translated into Irish by the middle of the fourteenth century. In recent years there has been a revival of the use of the old Gaelic language in Eire (Irish Republic). The Gaelic of the Scottish Highlands is closely related to this. The Scots had their own New Testament as early as 1767.

And herein lies an interesting tale. The Scottish Society for the Propagation of the Gospel opposed the use of the Scriptures in Gaelic. But the famous Samuel Johnson urged that "the holy books" should be given the people in their

[5]"Continental Versions to c. 1600," *The Cambridge History of the Bible: The West from the Reformation to the Present Day*, S. L. Greenslade, ed. (Cambridge: University Press, 1963), p. 103.

own language. He wrote: "To omit for a year, or for a day, the most efficacious method of advancing Christianity . . . is a crime." It took the great dictionary-maker to tell religious leaders what their duty was!

The large island of Iceland had the entire Bible in its Scandinavian tongue by 1584, thanks to King Frederick II of Denmark. He ordered every church to have a copy. The good bishop of the island arranged for the poorest people to receive free copies. The Iceland Bible Society was founded in 1815 and reported three years later that every family had either a Bible or a New Testament, which was read with diligence during the long winter evenings.

Parts of the New Testament were translated into at least three *Romani* dialects for the gypsies of central Europe. A gypsy who had made one translation became a Bible Society colporteur and then an evangelist. One of his high experiences took place at the grave of a fellow gypsy. After the Roman Catholic priest had conducted the service in unintelligible Latin, the colporteur stepped up and read the story of Lazarus ("I Am the Resurrection and the Life") in the familiar language of the people.

And so the Bible spread to all parts of Europe and to all classes of people. Today thousands of copies are going behind the iron curtain. *God's Smuggler,* by "Brother Andrew," is a thrilling story of how the Scriptures are being carried, at great risk of life, into all the Communist countries of eastern Europe.

Asia

It was in Asia that much of the Bible was written, and here many of the earliest translations were made. Among them were the Old Syriac (2nd cent.) and the Armenian (5th cent.), as well as the earlier Aramaic and Samaritan Targums.

A seeming tragedy is that the Scriptures were not translated into Arabic until a century after Mohammed's death. Had that "prophet" had the New Testament in his own language, how different might have been the religious history of Africa and Asia for the past 13 centuries!

The power of the printed word is one of the important factors in history. R. Kilgour writes:

> The Bible has been described as the unfettered missionary. It reaches where the Christian preacher is forbidden to enter. It knows no boundaries of closed lands. Human agents may be exluded, but the printed page finds its way in. Anti-Christian Governments may promulgate laws against it, may even confiscate existing copies; but the history of Christianity abundantly proves that nothing can wholly eradicate its message. In a most marvelous manner the Word of God liveth and abideth forever.[6]

This truth has been especially exemplified in the Himalayan area of central Asia. For centuries the four countries of Afghanistan, Tibet, Nepal, and Bhutan remained tightly closed against any Christian preachers. But at least parts of the Bible have been translated into all the main tribal tongues of these nations.

Nepal is a case in point. William Carey and his colleagues translated the New Testament into at least four dialects of this country. But it was not until 1914 that the whole Bible became available in Nepalese. Thousands of copies of Scripture found their way across the border into this forbidden land. Partly as a result of this, Christian missionaries are now at work in Nepal. Even in Tibet, "the roof of the world," the Bible is present in the language of the people.

It was in Nepal that Sadhu Sundar Singh lost his life, seeking to carry the gospel to these people. But he had already had a great ministry in India. Led to Christ himself

[6]*The Bible Throughout the World* (London: World Dominion Press, 1939), p. 107.

by reading the New Testament, he was always sharing it with the Hindus.

One day on a train he gave a copy of John's Gospel to another traveler. The man read a little in it, then tore it up and threw the pieces out the window.

Two years later Sadhu Sundar Singh learned that a seeker after truth had found these torn scraps of paper. On one fragment were the words "the Bread of Life." Hungering to know what this meant, he purchased a New Testament, was converted, and became a preacher of the gospel. Said Singh, "Really the torn pieces of St. John's Gospel proved to be a piece of the living Bread—the Bread of life."

The story of William Carey's translations of the Scriptures in India has already been told, though briefly. One incident might be added. When a Baptist mission was opened in Dacca in 1818, several villages were found in which the peasants called themselves *Satyagurus* (religious teachers). They showed the missionaries a much-worn Book, kept carefully in a wooden box. It was a copy of Carey's first Bengali New Testament, issued in 1801. Though the villagers did not know where it came from, they had found in it the new faith.

The Church of the Nazarene in India operates in a Marathi-speaking area. It is therefore of interest to know that the New Testament was translated into this language in 1811 and the whole Bible eight years later. This was another product of Carey's group at Serampore. Since then the Marathi Christians themselves have taken an active part in revising the translation for use today.

The Syrian Church of Malabar in southern India was conducting its services in Syriac, a foreign language, when a Protestant missionary arrived. The people spoke Malayalam, as they do today. So he made available a translation of the Gospels in their mother tongue.

The story of the Bible translation work done by Robert Morrison, the first Protestant missionary to China, is not as startling as that of William Carey in India. But it is a noble tale in its own right.

Morrison was only 10 years old when Carey launched his missionary enterprise in 1792. After some elementary instruction in the "three R's" (reading, writing, and 'rithmetic), he was apprenticed at a very early age to his father, who made lasts. His widow tells of his eagerness to study:

> For the purpose of securing a greater portion of quiet retirement, he had his bed removed to his workshop, where he would often pursue his studies until one or two in the morning. Even when at work, his Bible or some other book was placed open before him, that he might acquire knowledge or cherish the holy aspirations of spiritual devotion while his hands were busily occupied in the labors of life.[7]

At 19 years of age Morrison was ready be begin his study of Hebrew, Latin, and theology. It was not long until he felt a missionary concern and offered himself to the London Missionary Society. While at its mission school he studied Chinese with a resident of the town who had come from China. In 1807 he went to that distant land. As is well-known, Morrison labored for seven years before winning his first Chinese convert.

But meanwhile he was not idle. By 1814 he had a Chinese translation of the entire New Testament ready for the press. Another missionary had arrived in 1813 and perhaps helped Morrison finish the New Testament. At any rate, they worked together on the Old Testament translation and completed it in 1819.

In India over 200 languages and approximately 800 dialects are spoken. While the situation in China is much better, there are various dialects into which the Scriptures must be translated.

The story of one of these translations will serve to

---

[7] Quoted in McClintock and Strong, *op. cit.*, VI, 655.

illustrate the extreme dedication of translators to their task. It will also show the power of the Word.

On the Malabar coast of India a learned black Jew had translated the New Testament into Hebrew with the purpose of refuting Christianity. More than a century later a Jewish man in Russian Lithuania came across a Hebrew New Testament based on this. He read it and was converted. Emigrating to New York, he finally entered General Theological Seminary. He was such a brilliant linguist that he was offered a professorship there. But he declined it, saying that he was called to go to China to translate the Bible. Since the New Testament had already been published in Northern Mandarin, the missionary, Schereschewsky, tackled the Old Testament and finished it in four years.

But a sunstroke brought on a spinal disease which left him a complete invalid the rest of his life. All he could use was one finger of each hand. Lifted into his chair each morning, he worked for 25 years without quitting. With his two good fingers he tapped out his translation in Roman letters on a typewriter, and then his Chinese colleagues wrote it in Chinese characters. In this way he completed the Old Testament in another dialect, which already had the New Testament. And so the whole Bible was at last available to millions of people in their own tongue.

Africa

As a continent, Africa came of age later than some other global areas. As would be expected, Bible translation was tardy here. And yet this led the way in the development of literature. Kilgour writes:

> Most African languages were reduced to writing in the first instance with the express purpose of being the vehicle of teaching God's Word. Some piece of Scripture

is usually the earliest specimen of printing in these tongues.[8]

Once the work began, it moved forward rapidly. When the British and Foreign Bible Society was organized in 1804, only four African languages had any Scriptures in them. In 1876 this had gone to over 50, and by 1938 it was about 350.

Yet there are still many African tongues into which no part of the Bible has been translated. One authority lists the names of 366 Bantu dialects, and this is just one of the five main families of African speech.

The tragedy of the almost total eclipse of the Christian Church in North Africa is unparalleled in history. In the second, third, and fourth centuries Carthage was one of the great centers of Christianity. Even the temple of Venus in that city was turned into a Christian church. Among the great church fathers, Tertullian, Cyprian, and Augustine were North Africans. But the Moslem conquest of the seventh century left hardly a vestige of the Christian faith in this area, where the gospel had been preached so eloquently.

Why? Kilgour suggests one reason* that is worth considering. He says:

> The great warning from North Africa is that, alongside of preaching, there must be the Bible in the vernacular. Egypt, Syria, Armenia and Georgia prove that no Church which had the Scriptures in the speech of the common people has ever completely perished, and the task today is to repair the error which cost North Africa such a price.[9]

Samuel Zwemer, the leading authority on missions among the Moslems, tells of the visit of a colporteur to

[8]*Op. cit.,* pp. 33-34.
[9]*Ibid.,* p. 35.

Somaliland, in eastern Africa. Forty years later another man went there on the same errand. He found an old Arab who still had the Arabic Bible he had bought from the previous colporteur, still prayed the Lord's Prayer, and after 40 years had not forgotten the gospel message. Examples could be given from every continent of this power of the written Word to save men by the living Word.

Henry M. Stanley is well-known for his trip into Africa's jungles to find David Livingstone. One of the dramatic moments of history is the final meeting of the two men and Livingstone's refusal to return to civilization. The cry of Africa's heart held his heart in a viselike grip, and he could not leave.

What is not commonly known is that, with the help of an African boy and the king's scribe, Stanley was the first to translate a few verses of the Bible (the Ten Commandments) into the native language of Uganda. Then, in answer to his plea, the Church Missionary Society sent an emissary.

And now another hero steps onto the stage. Alexander Mackay, a brilliant young Scottish engineer, reduced Uganda's language to writing in 1880. With his own hands he cut out wooden type and printed portions of his new translation of Scripture. In spite of persecution that caused the murder of Bishop Hannington in October, 1885, the very next month Mackay printed 350 copies of the first sheets of Matthew. The work continued until the whole Bible was finished in 1896, six years after his death. In Uganda the term "reader" has come to mean "Christian."

One of the epics of missionary annals is the story of Madagascar. That island off the east coast of Africa had been entered by Roman Catholics with little success. When the Protestant missionaries came in 1818 they used an entirely different approach. The first thing they did was to translate God's Word into Malagasy, completing the entire Bible in 10 years.

But in 1835, when the church membership had reached about 200, the "killing times" began. The queen forbade anybody to possess the Christian Scriptures, on pain of death. Many who refused to give them up were tortured and killed.

Before the missionaries were expelled, they buried in the ground 70 copies of the Bible, and stored Scripture portions in other places, to be read by the persecuted Christians. Kilgour tells the result: "When the reign of terror ended after a quarter of a century, the little Church had increased tenfold, having been nourished, sustained, comforted and strengthened by one spiritual teacher, counsellor, friend and guide in this world and to the next, the Word of God which is able to make men wise unto Salvation." [10] Now the Christian Church includes hundreds of thousands and has sent missionaries to other areas.

Some 40 years ago there were exciting reports coming out of Africa about "Prophet Harris." Dressed in white robe and turban, he carried a rough wooden cross in his right hand and an English Bible in his left. In each town that he entered he placed the open Bible in the center of the crowd and denounced evil and idolatry. As a result of his preaching, British missionaries gathered many converts into churches and instructed them in Christianity. Investigation disclosed the fact that Harris had been born and brought up in a Liberian village where a pioneer missionary had translated the Scriptures into his mother tongue. It was this that apparently led him to become the flaming evangelist of later years.

In the Congo, missionaries worked for years to translate the Bible into a combined dialect, completing it in 1930. The effect of this on the Mongo tribe was tellingly illustrated within a short time. In 1894, at the funeral of a chief, 40 young men had been beheaded and their corpses buried

[10] *Ibid.*, p. 61.

with him. Many more than this were killed to provide for the feast that followed. But 40 years later (1934) there was a Communion service attended by some of the same people. Enemies who had formerly met only to kill and eat human flesh now sat together at the Lord's table. Instead of being armed with spears and knives, they carried their Bibles.

South America

In his book *Adventures with the Bible in Brazil*, Frederick Glass tells how as a colporteur he was selling Scriptures in a town. A farmer came to him, told him that he had purchased a copy of the Bible years before, and said, "I want you to come to my village." There the colporteur found a group of eager worshipers. The farmer had called in his friends and neighbors and read the Word of God to them. Soon many of them repented of their sins and were saved. Though they had never seen a white missionary or heard a Christian sermon, there were 11 converts who were ready for baptism. Finally a whole new Christian village was formed.

The main language of Brazil is Portuguese, whereas Spanish is used throughout most of the rest of the continent, together with Central America and Mexico. But there are hundreds of Indian tribes whose people speak their own native dialect. So the Wycliffe Translators are constantly at work, rendering the Word of God into the languages of the various tribes.

As an example, Dr. William Sedat, who translated the entire New Testament into the tongue of the Kekchi Indian tribe in Guatemala, gives John 14:1—"Let not your heart be troubled"—this way: "Don't shiver in your liver."

The Pacific Islands

Two Wesleyan missionaries landed in the Fiji Islands

in 1835. By 1864 they had translated the entire Bible into the leading Polynesian dialect. That very year the "Crier of War" drum called the people together. This time it was not for a cannibal feast, but to see the king, his family, and many warriors bow before the King of Kings. A month or two later the first Fiji edition of the Bible reached a neighboring island, and its king was converted. Twenty years after that the murder stone, on which victims' heads had been dashed, was hollowed into a baptismal font.

On one of the islands of the New Hebrides a missionary named John Geddie settled in 1848. At once he set to work translating the Gospel of Mark, which was published in 1853. Ten years later the New Testament appeared, and in 1879 the entire Bible. The epitaph on his tombstone reads as follows:

WHEN HE CAME IN 1848 THERE WAS NOT A CHRISTIAN;
WHEN HE DIED IN 1872 THERE WAS NOT A HEATHEN.

John G. Paton worked on another New Hebrides island, Aniwa. He too was concerned to give them the Bible in their mother tongue. But the frustrating fact was that there was no word in their language remotely resembling the great Christian concepts of grace and faith. How could you tell the people to believe on the Lord Jesus when there was no word for "believe"?

One day Paton was working in his hut on his new translation. A man came in. Weary with walking, he slumped down on a chair. As he did so he said, "I'm leaning my whole weight on this chair." Eagerly the missionary asked him to repeat the phrase. In that edition of the New Testament "believe" is translated "lean your whole weight on" —a good definition for all Christians!

Stories could be multiplied about the effect of God's Word on pagan people. But perhaps one more must suffice. The Maoris of New Zealand were known as especially fierce. But the Bible was finally completed in their language in 1924.

At a Communion service a missionary noticed a Maori withdraw from the altar and go back to his seat. After a while he returned and partook.

This was the man's explanation. He found himself before the Communion table kneeling beside a man who had killed his father and drunk his blood. He had sworn to kill this man the first time he saw him. Here are the man's words:

> So I went back to my seat. Then I saw in the spirit the upper sanctuary, and I seemed to hear a voice, "Hereby shall all men know that ye are my disciples, if ye love one another." And I saw another sight, a Cross and a Man nailed on it, and I heard Him say, "Father, forgive them, for they know not what they do." Then I went back to the altar.[11]

Questions

1. What man is considered the father of modern missions, and what contribution did he make to Bible translations?

2. What was the importance of Luther's translation of the Bible?

3. Why did the Church fail in North Africa?

4. What did Morrison do for the cause of missions in China?

5. What sacrifices did Alexander Mackay make in order to give the Bible to Uganda?

6. What effect has the Bible had in South America?

[11]*Ibid.*, p. 188.

VI

Its Communication

It took 80 years for the King James Version (1611) to win complete acceptance in the English-speaking world. Luther A. Weigle writes: "It was denounced as theologically unsound and ecclesiastically biased, as truckling to the king and unduly deferring to his belief in witchcraft, as untrue to the Hebrew text and relying too much on the Septuagint."[1] The translators themselves recognize in their Preface that every new translation is apt to be "glouted upon by every evil eye" and "gored by every sharp tongue." The Puritans in the British Isles and the Pilgrims in America clung tenaciously to their beloved Geneva Bible and were loath to give it up for this "newfangled" version.

But finally the King James Version became the dominant English Bible and held this position for over two centuries. This was largely because of its superior literary style, its Elizabethan prose.

But that is not the spoken or written language of our day. And so the twentieth century has seen an abundant crop of new English translations.

---

[1]"English Versions Since 1611," *Cambridge History of the Bible: The West from the Reformation to the Present Day*, S. L. Greenslade, ed. (Cambridge: University Press, 1963), p. 361.

Private Translations

These began much earlier, even in the seventeenth century. In 1645 the great Hebrew scholar, John Lightfoot, urged the House of Commons "to think of a review and survey of the translation of the Bible," that "the three nations [England, Ireland, Scotland] might come to understand the proper and genuine study of the Scriptures by an exact, vigorous, and lively translation."[2] Several paraphrases of the New Testament appeared soon after this.

a. *John Wesley's New Testament* (1755). The eighteenth century saw the appearance of several private translations, of which the most significant was that of John Wesley. In his preface, Wesley indicated that the King James Version needed improvement in three areas: a better Greek text, better interpretation, and better English. So concerned was he about this that he devoted his best energies to the task. He felt that this was an important factor in supporting and supplementing his preaching of scriptural salvation from all sin.

Wesley worked from the Greek New Testament, which had been his constant companion for many years. In line with his goal, he sought to establish the best Greek text available, making careful use of Bengel's *Gnomon*, which was published in Germany in 1742, based on Bengel's critical apparatus of 1734. In this respect Wesley was far ahead of most men of his day. He realized that Christian holiness demands honest scholarship, and he was earnest in his desire and arduous in his labors to discover the best Greek text and to translate it as accurately and clearly as possible.

Some years ago a careful study of *John Wesley's New Testament* indicated that it has 12,000 changes from the

[2]*Ibid.*, p. 363.

King James Version, many of them just matters of better English. In over 6,500 instances John Wesley's translation of the New Testament (1755) agreed with the Revised Standard Version (1946) against the King James Version (1611). In about 430 of these Wesley used a better Greek text than that on which the King James Version was based. This fact alone shows the real biblical scholarship of this preacher who desired to communicate the Word of God accurately and effectively to his generation. Unfortunately, too few of his professed adherents have followed fully in his trail.

During the nineteenth century private translations of the Bible were put out by such men as Noah Webster (1833), of dictionary fame, and Robert Young (1862), who compiled the great *Analytical Concordance of the Bible*. The latter made a very literal rendering of the original Hebrew and Greek. But neither of these translations had any permanent effect.

b. The Twentieth Century New Testament (1904). This was one of the first and best examples of a "modern-speech version." The wife of a Congregational minister in England worked much with children. She discovered that they could not understand the King James Version. So she began her own idiomatic translation of the Gospel of Mark. At the same time she wrote a letter to a scholarly magazine, asking for help on this project. The result was that over 30 people, from various walks of life, collaborated in a fresh rendering of the New Testament. The aim was to provide a translation for "working men and women, and children of all classes, a version which they could read without difficulty."[3] The result was the *Twentieth Century New Testament,* issued in three volumes (1898-1901) and finally revised in 1904.

[3]John H. P. Reumann, *The Romance of Bible Scripts and Scholars* (Englewood Cliffs, N.J.: Prentice-Hall, 1965), p. 166.

c. Weymouth's New Testament (1903). Richard Weymouth published in 1886 his *Resultant Greek Text*, in which he exhibited the text which had at that time been derived from the oldest and best Greek manuscripts. On the basis of this he sought to make "an idiomatic translation into everyday English." He called it *The New Testament in Modern Speech*.

This is still one of the most beautiful English translations that we can read. Here is a sample (John 21:15-17):

> When they had finished breakfast, Jesus asked Simon Peter,
> 'Simon, son of John, do you love me more than these others do?'
> 'Yes, Lord,' was his answer; 'you know that you are dear to me.'
> 'Then feed my lambs,' replied Jesus.
> Again a second time He asked him,
> 'Simon, son of John, do you love me?'
> 'Yes, Lord,' he said, 'you know that you are dear to me!'
> 'Then be a shepherd to my sheep,' he said.
> A third time Jesus put the question:
> 'Simon, son of John, am I dear to you?' . . .
> 'Lord,' he replied, 'you know everything, you can see that you are dear to me.'
> 'Then feed my sheep,' said Jesus.

Weymouth highlights the different verbs for "feed" and also the two words for "love." in his first two questions Jesus used *agapao*, which indicates the love of full loyalty. Peter had learned by his own betrayals of his Master that he did not have that kind of love. So he used a lesser term, *phileo*, which expresses affection or friendship. When Jesus, in His third question, dropped down to this lower word, it broke Peter's heart.

d. Moffatt's Bible (1926). James Moffatt was a Scottish scholar who taught at Union Theological Seminary in New York. In 1913 he issued *The New Testament: a New Trans-*

lation, and in 1926 a complete Bible (revised 1935). Because of his liberal views in biblical criticism, his translation was opposed by many. It does contain British terms that are unfamiliar to American readers. But it is one of the more readable English Bibles in print.

e. An American Translation (1939). In 1923, Edgar J. Goodspeed of the University of Chicago published his *American Translation* of the New Testament. It did for the United States what Moffatt's New Testament did for Britain. Based on the best Greek text available—Moffatt's judgment at this point was not so good—it forms a landmark in American translations. In some ways it is still the best. Weights, measurements, and money values are all given in contemporary American terms. The style is exceedingly readable.

In 1927 the Old Testament was added. This was the work of four scholars, with J. M. Powis Smith of the University of Chicago as editor. Finally, in 1939, there appeared *The Complete Bible: An American Translation,* including the Apocrypha as translated by Goodspeed.

f. Phillips' Translation (1958). In 1941 a vicar in the Church of England named J. B. Phillips was in charge of a large group of young people in southeast London. Night after night the enemy bombers swept in over the city in the terrible blitzes of that memorable winter.

Phillips tried reading the Bible to his parishioners to give them some assurance. But he found they had difficulty grasping the language of the King James Version. So he began making a fresh, idiomatic rendering of Paul's Epistles for their benefit. Immediately the Bible came alive.

The first Epistle he translated was Colossians. C. S. Lewis, the famous teacher of literature at both Oxford and Cambridge universities, saw a copy of this. Enthusiastically he wrote to Phillips: "It is like seeing an old picture which has been cleaned." He encouraged him to keep up his work. The result was the publication of *Letters to Young Churches* in 1948.

J. B. Phillips had a genius for saying the right thing in the right way. We can cite only a few examples. His translation of I Cor. 8:2 reads: "For whatever a man may know, he still has a lot to learn." Here is another: "I am no shadowboxer; I really fight!" (I Cor. 9:26b) And: "I have worked harder than any of the others" (15:10c). Quoted frequently is this: "Don't let the world around you squeeze you into its own mold" (Rom. 12:2).

These samples underscore what ought to be an obvious truth: that every good translation, especially a freer one, constitutes a form of commentary. The more of these modern-speech translations one reads, the more fresh insights into Scripture he will get. The practice of reading a different translation of the New Testament each year in one's private devotions will greatly increase a person's knowledge of the Word of God. At the rate of a chapter a day, the New Testament can be read through in less than a year.

In 1952, Phillips published *The Gospels*. Because the language of the four Gospels is not as difficult as that of Paul's Epistles, this volume is not as striking in its new wordings. This was also true, in lesser measure, of *The Young Church in Action* (1955), a translation of Acts. *The Book of Revelation* followed in 1957 and the entire New Testament in one volume in 1958. It is deservedly one of the most popular one-man versions in print.

g. The Berkeley Version (1959). In 1945 a Baptist named Gerrit Verkuyl put out his translation of the New Testament, which won wide acceptance among evangelical Christians. Because it was published at Berkeley, Calif., it was called the Berkeley Version. With the help of some 20 scholars the Old Testament was translated, and *The Holy Bible: The Berkeley Version in Modern English* appeared in 1959. The translation, on the whole, is very helpful, though some footnotes are highly subjective.

h. Beck's New Testament (1963). Among the very readable translations of recent years is *The New Testament in the Language of Today,* by William Beck. It is published by the Concordia Publishing House. The style is thoroughly contemporary and often striking. For instance, II Cor. 7:2 reads: "Make room in your hearts for us. We haven't wronged anyone, ruined anyone, gotten the best of anyone."

i. The Living New Testament (1967). This first appeared in three installments. As in the case of Phillips' translation, the volume of the Epistles, *Living Letters,* appeared first (1962). It immediately caught fire. Teen-agers especially enjoyed reading it, and it made the difficult passages in Paul's Epistles live for all ages. *Living Gospels* and *Living Prophecies* completed the New Testament. The Old Testament has recently been completed and the entire *Living Bible* published (1971).

All these volumes were published anonymously by the Tyndale House of Wheaton, Ill. But now it is common knowledge that Kenneth Taylor is the main translator.

This new version is openly described on the title page as "Paraphrased." And that it is. Actually, it is such a free rendering in many places that it is highly interpretive. This is both an asset and a liability. If the interpretation is correct it adds to the reader's understanding. But, by the same token, if the interpretation should be wrong the reader is led astray. For this reason most evangelical scholars prefer a translation that is a bit more conservative; that is, one that sticks a little more closely to the Greek text.

j. Today's English Version (1968). Carrying the appealing title, *Good News for Modern Man,* sporting a striking cover of newspaper mastheads, and selling for an absurdly low price, this paperback volume has had a phenomenal sale. It was not long after publication until the figure passed the 10-million mark. Around the world it is widely read, promoted by the American Bible Society.

Dr. Bratcher had already put out his *Translator's Handbook on the Gospel of Mark.* His aim in his new translation was obviously to make it as readable as a newspaper. In this he succeeded well.

However, his handling of individual passages is not always a happy one. Especially objectionable is his translation of *sarx* (flesh) as "human nature." So the human nature is to be destroyed—which is obvious nonsense.

But even with these faults, we can rejoice that the New Testament is being read in TEV by many people who would otherwise pass it by. We thank God for this.

Committee Translations

We have already told the story of Tischendorf's discovery of the Sinaitic manuscript of the Greek Bible in 1859. About the same time he publicized the only other known Greek manuscript from the fourth century, Vaticanus. This had been kept hidden away in the Vatican Library at Rome, but Tischendorf gained access to it and revealed the nature of its contents. Today it is widely considered to be the most valuable single manuscript of the Greek New Testament. The fifth-century manuscript Alexandrinus reached England in 1627, just a few years too late to be used by the King James translators.

Unfortunately, the Greek text which these translators used was essentially that of Erasmus. He had half a dozen Greek manuscripts in all—two of the Gospels, two of Paul's Epistles, one for Acts and the General Epistles, and one for Revelation. In the case of the last one the final verses were missing. Undaunted, Erasmus translated these last verses of Revelation from the Latin. And none of his manuscripts was earlier than the tenth century. In other words, the King James Version of the New Testament is based on a late medieval Greek text.

In contrast to this, today we have over 5,000 Greek manuscripts of the New Testament, in whole or in part. And these reach back to the ninth, eighth, seventh, sixth, fifth, and fourth centuries—and, in the case of the papyri, to the beginning of the third century (about the year A.D. 200).

a. The Revised Version (1885). On the basis of these older manuscripts, Westcott and Hort were laboring diligently to construct a better Greek text (they did not have the papyri). Increasingly scholars realized the need for a new revision of the Bible.

Finally, at the Convocation of Canterbury in 1870 the decision was made to revise the King James Version. Old and New Testament companies were appointed. Altogether 65 British scholars participated in this project. Included were not only members of the Church of England, Church of Scotland, and Church of Ireland, but also Baptists, Methodists, Congregationalists, and Presbyterians. The New Testament was published on May 17, 1881, and a special copy presented to Queen Victoria. The entire Revised Bible appeared in 1885.

The New Testament company had met in the Jerusalem Chamber of Westminster Abbey. Prominent in this group were Westcott and Hort. Their *New Testament in Greek* did not appear until a few days later in 1881, but they made advance sheets available to the revisers as they worked. So the new version was based on a sound Greek text.

Other great scholars in the New Testament company were J. B. Lightfoot, whose commentaries on the Greek text of Paul's Epistles are still invaluable, and W. Milligan, W. F. Moulton, and F. H. A. Scrivener.

Within a few days 2 million copies of the Revised New Testament were sold, and about 3 million altogether the first year. On May 20, 1881, the new version arrived in New York. Two days later the entire New Testament was reprinted in both the *Chicago Tribune* and the *Chicago Times*. The *Tribune* employed 92 compositors and five correctors, and is said to have completed setting up the type in 12 hours.

2. *The American Standard Version* (1901). The British invited American cooperation in the revision, so an American Committee of Revisers was set up with Philip Schaff as chairman. Beginning in 1872, correspondence was carried on between the two groups. Some American suggestions were adopted, while others were set aside. But the American revisers wanted more drastic changes than their British brethren did. For instance, they very wisely wanted "Holy Ghost" changed to "Holy Spirit," since *ghost* now means the spirit of a dead person. They also desired the elimination of some other archaic words and phrases.

Finally it was decided to put out a separate edition in the United States. Its official name was "The American Standard Edition of the Revised Version," but it is more commonly known as the American Standard Version (ASV). It came out on August 26, 1901.

The English and American editions shared a common fault. Both Spurgeon and Schaff are credited with having summed it up in this way: "It is strong in Greek, weak in English." This is shown by the fact that it became a favorite "pony" for students to use in translating the Greek New Testament in school. For this reason the Revised Version was not suitable for reading in public. It was good for study but not for worship, so it did not gain great popularity. However, the American Standard Version was more widely accepted in the United States than the Revised Version was in Britain. The latter has rarely been read in British churches.

Though the King James Version has been rightly recognized as "the noblest monument of English prose," it became increasingly clear that it did not meet the need of twentieth-century readers. As we have seen, it was based on a poor Greek text. Furthermore, many of its English words have changed their meanings since 1611 (the period of Shakespeare). Over 800 words and phrases in the King James Version are not used in the same sense today, and of these about 200 mean something radically different. *The Bible Word Book*, by Ronald Bridges and Luther Weigle,[4] gives a careful discussion of 827 such terms, arranged in alphabetical order.

The most serious problem is that some words in the King James Version now mean exactly the opposite of what they did in 1611. The writer once heard a preacher take as his text, "I will work, and who shall let it?" (Isa. 43:13) He proceeded to deliver a message on consecration: "God wants to work; who will let Him work in your heart and life?" A glance at the context of this passage in Isaiah shows that God is challenging the false gods of the people. What the text really means is: "I *will* work, and who's going to stop Me?" The Hebrew verb translated "let" actually means "to hinder."

The same thing is true in II Thess. 2:7—"Only he who now letteth will let, until he be taken out of the way." The Greek clearly says "restrains," not "letteth." In other words, when the King James Version was made, "let" could mean "not allow"; now it means "allow." Obviously a translation of the Bible which in some places tells the reader today exactly the opposite of what the original Greek or Hebrew says does not correctly communicate the truth of God's Word.

In Phil. 1:8 the King James Version has Paul saying, "How greatly I long after you all in the bowels of Jesus Christ." One wonders what happens in the minds of people

[4](New York: Thomas Nelson and Sons, 1960).

sitting in church when they hear that read from the pulpit. At best, they are repelled by the vulgarity of using such an expression in public; at worst, their thoughts are apt to take them down a dead-end side street contemplating the physical meaning of the term. Today translators wisely render the phrase, "with the affection of Christ Jesus."

The same problem occurs three times in the short letter to Philemon. The King James Version reads: "The bowels of the saints are refreshed by thee" (v. 7); "Therefore receive him, that is, mine own bowels" (v. 12); "Refresh my bowels in the Lord" (v. 20). The ancients thought of the seat of the affections as the bowels; we place it in the heart. Obviously "heart" is the correct translation in these three passages, and they should always be read that way in public.

Examples of similar misleading translations in the King James Version could be cited almost endlessly. John the Seer did not have "admiration" for the scarlet woman (Rev. 17:6). The Greek word simply means "amazement." In Rom. 7:15, "allow" means "understand," not permit or approve. Paul's statement, "I know nothing by myself" (I Cor. 4:4), really means, "I know nothing *against* myself" —which is quite a different matter. "By and by" is used in Mark 6:25 and Luke 21:9 where the Greek clearly says "immediately," just the opposite of "by and by" in our usage today.

There are instances also where the translators of the King James Version were inaccurate in handling the Greek. "Drink ye all of it" (Matt. 26:27), is repeated thousands of times in Communion services every year. So the communicants obediently drink all the juice in their little glasses. But the Greek clearly says: "All of you drink of it." When Jesus inaugurated the Lord's Supper in the Upper Room the disciples, at His invitation, all drank from a common cup. The common cup is still used by some Christian groups, but in recent years most communions have substituted individual glasses for sanitary reasons. But the correct wording should still be used: "All of you drink of it." This is what Communion is—not each individual draining his glass, but all partaking together.

The same mistake in using "all" as an object rather than as a part of the subject (the Greek has the nominative case rather than the accusative) is found in Jas. 3:2—"For in many things we offend all." That says that we offend all people. But the Greek says: "For we all offend." That is, we all sometimes offend others by something we say or do; we all make mistakes. But we certainly do not offend everybody!

If we are honestly concerned that people should know the truth of God's saving Word, we shall seek to give them a translation that says clearly in today's language what the inspired Greek and Hebrew originals actually say. This is what has been attempted in recent translations.

c. The Revised Standard Version (1952). The American Standard Version (1901) was not really a twentieth-century translation. It still retained the *eth* endings on verbs. The language was far different from the English that is spoken today.

So in 1937 the International Council of Religious Education voted to authorize a revision of the 1901 version. This revision was to "embody the best results of modern scholarship as to the meaning of the Scriptures, and express this meaning in English diction which is designed for use in public and private worship and preserves those qualities which have given to the King James Version a supreme place in English literature."

Thirty-two scholars worked countless hours, without any financial remuneration. The New Testament committee convened a total of 145 days, besides all the time spent in making the basic translations before the meetings. The New

Testament of the Revised Standard Version was published in 1946 and the complete Bible in 1952.

In both years a storm of protest swept across the country. Most of it was due to misinformation or ignorance of the facts. Probably 95 percent of the critical statements were simply not true. For instance, the allegation was widely printed that the RSV translators had "taken the Blood out of the New Testament" because they did not believe in the atoning sacrifice of Christ. A frequently printed statement said that they had "omitted the Blood in many passages in the New Testament." But the accusers could cite only one passage, Col. 1:14, where "through his blood" is left out in the Revised Standard Version. And the only reason the translators omitted it is that it is not in any of the early Greek manuscripts. Some later scribe had inserted it here from Eph. 1:7, where it is a genuine reading in the Greek. The RSV translators had to be honest in translating what they found in the Greek text.

Another accusation was that the RSV denies the deity of Jesus because it has the centurion at the Cross saying, "Truly this man was a son of God" (Mark 15:39), instead of "the Son of God." But the Greek does not have the definite article. Furthermore, Luke reports the centurion as saying, "Certainly this was a righteous man" (Luke 23:47), which is exactly what "a son of God" means. The Roman centurion, with his pagan religion, did not have any background for confessing the deity of Jesus!

Actually, this doctrine is stated in the RSV just as clearly as in the KJV. What the critics did not bother to say was that the deity of Jesus is definitely declared in the RSV rendering of Titus 2:13—"our great God and Savior Jesus Christ" (Christ is both God and Saviour)—where it is not stated in the KJV: "the great God and our Saviour Jesus Christ" (two separate persons). If the RSV translators were trying to deny the deity of Jesus, why did they put it in where the King James Version does not have it?

d. The New English Bible (1970). In 1961 the New Testament of *The New English Bible* appeared. Unlike the RSV, it was not a revision but a new translation. This was wise. Revisions are always less than ideal.

The New English Bible has a freshness and vigor that is positively refreshing. In many places it makes delightful reading. Inevitably there are passages that will not please some people. No translation can avoid this fate, for no translation can possibly be perfect. Probably the main justifiable criticism that can be made of the NEB is that it paraphrases too freely at times and introduces a few interpretations that might be objectionable. But it, like most translations, can be used helpfully.

The translating was done by the best scholars of Britain. *The New English Bible*, complete with Apocrypha, was published by the Oxford and Cambridge University presses in 1970.

e. The New American Standard Bible. This is a revision of the American Standard Version of 1901, seeking to put it in up-to-date English. The New Testament appeared in 1963. It is an excellent translation made entirely by scholars who are thoroughly evangelical. In fact, we do not hesitate to recommend it as the best study version of the New Testament in English. If one wants to know exactly what the Greek text says, he will usually find it here. The Old Testament was published in 1971 by the Lockman Foundation, producers of the well-known *Amplified Bible*.

f. The New American Bible (1970). The Catholic Biblical Association of America has made an excellent translation of the entire Bible from the original Hebrew, Aramaic, and Greek. It was sponsored by the Bishop's Committee of the Confraternity of Christian Doctrine, and is the first official Catholic Bible in English that is made from the original languages. We are grateful for this new version intended to encourage American Catholics to read their Bibles.

g. *A Contemporary Translation.* As we have noted, the NASB is a translation for study purposes, as well as devotional reading. Its one weakness, perhaps, is that if follows the policy that every Greek word must be represented in English. This results, for instance, in the frequent repetition, in the Gospels, of the expression "answered and said." Today we would simply say "answered."

So some years ago a group of about 40 scholars met by invitation in Chicago. Out of this meeting a committee of 14 was appointed to plan for a new, fresh translation in contemporary English. It would be made by evangelical scholars. The writer is honored to be a member of the committee. Our aim is to see that the finished product will be thoroughly acceptable to the entire evangelical constituency in the United States. The translation is to be published by the New York Bible Society International. It is hoped that the New Testament will be available in 1973 and the Old Testament a few years later.

Few people have any idea of the immense amount of work involved in making a careful translation of the Bible. I did the basic translation of Matthew, Mark, and Luke over a period of three years, consulting some with colleagues. This was sent to the executive secretary, Dr. Edwin Palmer. He checked it over and made many suggestions for changes. I then spent six days, 10 hours a day, working with an Intermediate Editorial Committee on Mark's Gospel, two weeks on Matthew, and three weeks on Luke. The results went through a General Editorial Committee, meeting for several weeks at a later date. The translator was then allowed to react to GEC suggested changes. Finally the Committee on Bible Translation, which has ultimate responsibility for the translation, voted on each proposed change. This is the way each book of the Bible is being handled.

Hopefully this will be a truly contemporary translation that all evangelicals can use with confidence.

Questions

1. What is the significance of John Wesley's translation of the New Testament?

2. What is the difference between Moffatt's and Goodspeed's translations?

3. What is the main value of Phillips' translation?

4. How would you compare *Good News for Modern Man* (TEV) and the *Living New Testament?*

5. What were the main reasons for revising the King James Version?

6. Compare *The New American Standard Bible* with the projected *A Contemporary Translation*, as far as their objectives and methods are concerned.

Epilogue

Perhaps the author may be allowed to give a word of personal testimony. It was on Nov. 3, 1922, that I accepted Jesus Christ as my Saviour and Lord, at the close of a Bible study class in a Friends academy. For years I had prayed regularly in family worship and attended church faithfully. My outward life was above reproach. But that day the Holy Spirit through the Word convicted me of the fact that I was a sinner in God's sight.

One of the first fruits of conversion was a new love for God's Word. In the intervening 50 years the Bible has been my daily Companion, giving continual guidance and strength.

There have been three stages in my study of the Bible. The first was a thorough acquaintance with the King James Version in my daily devotions and in intensive study of the English Bible for two years in a Bible school.

The second stage was the study of the Greek and Hebrew originals in college, seminary, and university. This has eventuated in 40 years of teaching the Greek and English New Testament in college and seminary, as well as writing about a dozen commentaries on books of the New Testament, all based on a careful study of the Greek text. In the last few years my main concentration has been on the translating of the New Testament.

Meanwhile a third stage took place. I discovered that there was a richness of meaning to be found in reading the many helpful translations that have appeared in this century. No single translation that has come out in print gives the best rendering of every verse. For various passages in the New Testament one will find the clearest and richest rendering in Weymouth or Goodspeed, in Berkeley or Beck, in the NASB or ACT. Paul says: "That ye . . . may be able to comprehend with all saints what is the breadth, and length, and depth, and height" (Eph. 3:18). Different translators get varying insights into the meaning of particular passages. The student of the Bible will go deeper and higher, wider and farther in his understanding of the Word as he uses different translations.

One word more. This deepening and broadening of Bible study has not robbed me of that early love for the Word of God. Rather, it has deepened my devotion to it and increased the conviction that the Bible is the inspired Word of God.

The miracle of the Bible is that, though written by many men over a period of a millennium and a half, it has a single message throughout—divine redemption. From Genesis to Revelation it says that man has sinned, a holy God cannot condone sin, but God's love guarantees that He will forgive those who turn to Him in repentance and faith. And that message comes through today just as clearly as it did nearly 2,000 years ago.